PRAISE FOR *SOUL CRY*

How do we live in this broken world where everything is shaking and becoming more unstable each day? You feel it, don't you? From the nightly news to social media, we live in a world that appears to be coming more unhinged. Author Gary Roe offers daily help as our souls cry out for comfort, perspective, and stability in this uncertain world. As Gary says, "In a world that is at war and falling apart, our souls need to vent in God's direction." He has prepared a resource that helps train our souls to cry out to the Lord daily. *Soul Cry* offers daily prayers grounded in God's truth to help us express our hearts' desires to the Lord.

I count it one of my great privileges to know Gary Roe and to personally benefit from his ministry of comfort for the hurting and compassion for the grieving. In his numerous books and in his speaking ministry, Gary provides help for those suffering loss and tenderness for us whom this broken world has wounded.

Daily working through this treasure of support will enable followers of Jesus to keep their feet firmly planted in Him and in His stabilizing support. I highly endorse this three-month journey.

—Reggie Coe, Pastor

Refreshing. When life's chaos distracts and discourages, these short, inspiring devotions will help you refocus and recharge. In *Soul Cry*, Roe addresses our need for God's help and comfort in our challenges.

—Charles Page, MD,
author of *A Spoonful of Courage for the Sick and Suffering*

Soul Cry is a book on grief that touches all the places of the heart and mind. Having suffered many losses, including the deaths of two husbands, I wish I had had this book to read when I was going through the darkest parts of grief. Even now it speaks to me of a continuing journey I am on with Jesus. I commend Gary Roe for his ongoing work to help others and his vulnerability in sharing his own losses. I believe this book should be given to everyone who has suffered a loss.

—Terezihna H. Augustine DHM, Ph.D.

Gary Roe has responded to the *Soul Cry* of those who are grieving. Each chapter is loaded with ointment to soothe the aching of the grieving heart. This book is a must-read for both those who are grieving and those who provide bereavement ministries.

—Brian Kenney, Pastor & Chaplain

I have been moved, challenged, encouraged, and incredibly blessed by *Soul Cry*. When my words fail, and my prayers seem so understated, Gary's honest insight and Biblical basis of each writing with relevant Scripture have carried my prayers in a deep, heartfelt manner. You will be blessed with these readings and will use this book again and again when facing life's difficulties.

—Lynette McCombs,
Widow's Outreach Ministry Facilitator

Soul Cry is like a daily companion that helps the reader walk through the hardest period of the grieving process. The words provide comfort and a clear path to healing. As someone who has lost loved ones, I'm grateful for this resource.

—Kelli Levey Reynolds, widow, writer

SOUL CRY

DEVOTIONAL PRAYERS FOR WOUNDED, GRIEVING, AND SUFFERING HEARTS

GARY ROE

Soul Cry: Devotional Prayers for Wounded,
Grieving, and Suffering Hearts
Copyright © 2023 by Gary Roe
All rights reserved.
First Edition: 2023

Print ISBN: 978-1-950382-81-1
eBook ISBN: 978-1-950382-82-8
Hardcover ISBN: 978-1-950382-83-5
Large Print ISBN: 978-1-950382-84-2

Cover and Formatting: Streetlight Graphics

Published by: Healing Resources Publishing

Bible references are from:

The author is not engaged in rendering medical or psychological
services, and this book is not intended as a guide to diagnose or
treat medical or psychological problems. If you require medical,
psychological, or other expert assistance, please seek the services
of your own physician or mental health professional.

OTHER BOOKS BY GARY ROE

THE GOD AND GRIEF SERIES:

Grief Walk: Experiencing God After the Loss of a Loved One

Widowed Walk: Experiencing God After the Loss of a Spouse

Broken Walk: Experiencing God After the Loss of a Child

Orphaned Walk: Experiencing God After the Loss of a Parent (Coming Soon)

THE COMFORT SERIES:

Comfort for Grieving Hearts: Hope and Encouragement in Times of Loss

Comfort for the Grieving Spouse's Heart: Hope and Healing After Losing Your Partner

Comfort for the Grieving Parent's Heart: Hope and Healing After Losing Your Child

Comfort for the Grieving Adult Child's Heart: Hope and Healing After Losing Your Parent

THE GOOD GRIEF SERIES:

The Grief Guidebook: Common Questions,
Compassionate Answers, Practical Suggestions

Shattered: Surviving the Loss of a Child

Hope in a World Gone Mad: Finding
God in Grief, Fear, and Anxiety

Aftermath: Picking Up the Pieces After a Suicide

Teen Grief: Caring for the Grieving Teenage Heart

Please Be Patient, I'm Grieving: How to Care
for and Support the Grieving Heart

Heartbroken: Healing from the Loss of a Spouse

Surviving the Holidays Without You:
Navigating Loss During Special Seasons

GRIEVING THE WRITE WAY SERIES

Grieving the Write Way: Journal and Workbook

Grieving the Write Way for Siblings:
A Practical Grief Workbook

THE DIFFERENCE MAKER SERIES:

Difference Maker: Overcoming Adversity and Turning
Pain into Purpose, Every Day (Adult & Teen Editions)

Living on the Edge: How to Fight and Win the Battle
for Your Mind and Heart (Adult & Teen Editions)

Thank you for purchasing *Soul Cry.*

I hope and pray that you will find this book of Scripture-based devotional prayers comforting, healing, encouraging, and hope-giving.

Please don't read this book just once.

Read it again and again.

Let these Scriptures bathe your heart and soul.

If you do not have a relationship with Jesus Christ (or aren't sure if you do), please read the brief *Receiving Jesus and His Life* explanation on page 301.

As a thanks for purchasing *Soul Cry,*

please accept this free gift (eBook, PDF):

*What in the World is Going On
(And What's Coming Next)?*

Download yours today:

https://www.garyroe.com/what-in-the-world/

WHAT *SOUL CRY* IS ALL ABOUT

Our souls are crying out.

The world is shaking. Things are changing rapidly, and not for the better.

Conflict. Dissension. Division. Anger. Rage. Hatred.

Lack of common decency and respect. Threats. Violence. Lawlessness.

Wars and rumors of wars. Food shortages and famine. Natural disasters. Destruction. Illness. Disease. Death.

Then there are all of our personal stresses and losses.

Jobs. Vocations. Careers. Increasing inflation. Diminishing savings. Rising taxes. Crushing debt.

Relational conflicts. Family fragmentation. Strained friendships. Estrangements.

Then there's the incredible, painful, and often traumatic loss of people we love and care about - friends, neighbors, family members, siblings, spouses, children, grandchildren.

It can seem like everything is falling apart.

We need to vent about all this. More than this, we need to vent in God's direction. Our souls need to cry out to Him - honestly and authentically.

This is what *Soul Cry* is all about.

WHAT YOU NEED TO KNOW ABOUT *SOUL CRY*

Before you get started, here are some things you need to know about this book:

WHAT IS *SOUL CRY*?

Soul Cry is a book of prayers which are grounded in the Bible and designed to connect with your soul. Each chapter contains a prayer based on a Bible verse or passage. These prayers are brief - about 2-3 pages long.

WHO IS THIS *SOUL CRY* WRITTEN FOR?

Soul Cry was written for followers of Jesus who are grieving and suffering from all the loss and change in their own lives and in the world around them. The goal of *Soul Cry* is to help wounded hearts cry out to God amid the pain, chaos, and upheaval that surrounds them.

HOW DO I READ *SOUL CRY*? STRAIGHT THROUGH? CAN I JUMP AROUND BASED ON THE CHAPTER TITLE?

Soul Cry was designed to be read straight through, one chapter a day. The book contains daily prayers for three months, with 31 prayers for each month.

In essence, *Soul Cry* is a daily prayer devotional.

Of course, you are free to read *Soul Cry* in whatever order you wish. I would encourage you, however, not to try and control where you read based on what you think you need. Rather, trust the Lord that He knows what you need on any particular day. Rest in Him.

When you read, listen. God speaks through His Word.

SOME CHAPTERS HAVE LORD IN ALL CAPS. WHAT'S THE SIGNIFICANCE OF THIS?

In the Old Testament, LORD in all caps is a translation of the Hebrew YHWH.

In Exodus 3, when Moses asked God His name, God responded, "I AM WHO I AM. This is what you are to say to the Israelites: 'I AM has sent me to you.'"

"I AM" in this verse is YHWH.

Vowels were added and YHWH became Yahweh so that this name might be able to be pronounced. Every instance in the Old Testament where you see LORD, you are reading the personal name by which God revealed Himself - YHWH or Yahweh.

Included in this awesome name are these basic truths:

- He is the Eternal One, without beginning and without end, who has always been and will always be.
- He has life in Himself and needs nothing.
- He is the Almighty, Infinite, and Sovereign Creator who is completely free to do as He pleases and wills.
- He reveals Himself and seeks relationship with His creation (especially people who are created in His image), not because He needs us but out of love for us because we need Him.

What an awesome name!

EACH CHAPTER ENDS WITH "IN JESUS' NAME..." WHY DON'T YOU END WITH "AMEN"? AND WHY THE ELLIPSIS?

This is just my personal preference. When I pray, either silently or aloud, I end with "In Jesus' name" and almost never say "Amen." I try to take seriously God's command to us in 1

Thessalonians 5:17 to, "Pray without ceasing." Leaving off the "Amen" is my way of saying, "This prayer is ongoing. I want to live a life of prayer."

Why the ellipsis? Again, my personal preference. I tend to think visually, so when I say, "In Jesus' name," my brain actually adds those three dots. That's me saying, "This prayer is to be continued in my life today..."

WHO ARE YOU TO WRITE A BOOK LIKE THIS?

I am follower of Jesus Christ. I come from a background of heavy loss and sexual abuse. I came to Jesus when I was 11 years old. Though I didn't know it, everything changed in that moment.

As losses and wounds continued to pile up, God faithfully brought me through them one by one. He comforted, encouraged, and healed me, even though many times I was in so much pain I could not even sense His presence. At least four times in my life I thought, "That's it. I'm not going to make it through this." Obviously, I was wrong. God is faithful indeed.

In high school and college, my plan was to become a physician. God had other plans. I became a trained theologian with two seminary degrees. Over the past four decades I've had the privilege of serving Jesus as a church-planting missionary in Japan, a pastor of several churches in Texas and Washington, and a hospice chaplain and grief counselor. I now serve as an author, Bible teacher, grief specialist, and grief coach.

Jesus is life. He is my life. It's an honor to serve Him by writing.

DO YOU HAVE ANY OTHER INPUT FOR ME BEFORE I BEGIN TO READ?

Please don't get in a hurry. In fact, hurry will be a major hindrance to your prayer life.

Take your time. Ask God to speak to you before you begin reading. As you read, feel free to stop, think, and meditate on the Scriptures and what's being said.

And, as I mentioned before, when you read, listen. God is speaking through what He has already spoken. As Paul shared with us in 2 Timothy 3:16, *"All Scripture is God-breathed and profitable to teaching, for reproof, for correction, and for training in righteousness."*

God is speaking today. Are we listening?

I have prayed for you as you read *Soul Cry*. I will continue to pray for you.

In fact, let me pray for you now:

Lord, thank you for the person reading these words. Remind them that You created them in Your image. You thought of them before You created the universe. You planned them. When the time was right, You personally knit them together in their mother's womb. You created them unique in all of human history, even if they're a twin. Two thousand years ago, Jesus Christ went to the cross thinking about them. Your love for them is infinite and perfect. You have a plan for them, and You are working out that plan.

Lord, I ask that You comfort them through this book. Bring healing. Give perspective and hope. Deepen and increase their faith and trust in You. Empower them to yield to You all and everything, so that they might live in the freedom You have already given them in Christ. Teach them who they are - who they really are.

Lord Jesus, You willingly gave Your life for them, so that You could give Your life to them, so that You could live Your life in and through them. Over time, give them intimacy with You that they never thought possible. Fill them with Your Spirit and empower them to keep in step with Your Spirit.

I pray now what Paul prayed for the Christ followers in Ephesus:

For this reason I bow my knees before the Father, from whom every family in heaven and on earth is named, that according to the riches of his glory he may grant you to be strengthened with power through his Spirit in your inner being, so that Christ may dwell in your hearts through faith—that you, being rooted and grounded in love, may have strength to comprehend with all the saints what is the breadth and length and height and depth, and to know the love of Christ that surpasses knowledge, that you may be filled with all the fullness of God.

(Ephesians 3:14-19)

May it be so, Lord.

In Jesus' name...

If you do not have a relationship with Jesus Christ or aren't sure if you do, please read the brief *Receiving Jesus and His Life* explanation on page 301.

THE FIRST MONTH

DAY 1

A Dry Place
Psalm 63:1-8

You, God, are my God, earnestly I seek You;
I thirst for You, my whole being longs for You,
in a dry and parched land where there is no water.
(63:1)

I am shaken, O God.
I don't know what to think.
I don't know what to do.
How could this happen?
I seek You. I long for You.
This wilderness threatens to undo me.
My heart cries out for You.
You are greater than all wildernesses.

I have seen you in the sanctuary
and beheld your power and your glory.
Because your love is better than life,
my lips will glorify you.
(63:2-3)

I have experienced Your goodness.
You have blessed me immeasurably.
I cling to You and Your love for me.
LORD, reassure my stunned and shaken heart.
May I choose to praise and give thanks,
even now, even here.

I will praise you as long as I live,
and in your name I will lift up my hands.
I will be fully satisfied as with the richest of foods;
with singing lips my mouth will praise you.
(63:4-5)

Now is not forever.
Help me to remember this.
This too will pass, though I don't know how or when.
I have You. I will always have You.
You will lead me through this painful, barren place.
You will meet my needs.

On my bed I remember you;
I think of you through the watches of the night.
Because you are my help,
I sing in the shadow of your wings.
I cling to you;
your right hand upholds me.
(63:6-8)

I rest in You, my Lord and my God.

I trust You.

Help me to trust You more.

In Jesus' name…

DAY 2

Loved, But Lonely
Psalm 23:1-6

O Lord, Creator and Sustainer of all,
I come to You again today.
You are always with me.
You are here, now.

My heart aches, my soul hurts.
I am consumed with grief and longing.
I am loved, but lonely, so lonely.
Hear my heart, O Perfect Father.

The LORD is my shepherd.
I lack nothing.
He makes me lie down in green pastures,
He leads me beside quiet waters,
He restores my soul.
(23:1-2)

I know that if I have You, I have everything.
I know this, LORD,

even as I am trudging through this pain.

You take care of me.

You provide for me.

You are at work in me.

You renew me from the inside out.

You guide me along the right paths for Your name's sake.
Even though I walk through the darkest valley,
I will fear no evil, for You are with me;
Your rod and your staff, they comfort me.
(23:3-4)

I will let You guide me.

I will follow You.

You walk with me in this darkness.

This place is not dark to You.

You are my constant companion,

always, each and every moment.

My Lord, my shepherd, my guide, my protector.

You comfort me.

Comfort me, O Lord.

You prepare a table before me
in the presence of my enemies
You anoint my head with oil;
my cup overflows.
(23:5)

You provide for me in unusual ways.
You lift me up.
You bless me continually.
Open my eyes to see You and Your blessings.
Though I feel as if I have next to nothing,
remind me that my cup is always overflowing.

Surely your goodness and love will
follow me all the days of my life,
and I will dwell in the house of the LORD forever.
(23:6)

I do not have to chase Your love and goodness,
for you are always loving and always good,
every day, all day.
Sustain me when my heart trembles,
when my soul goes numb.
You are with me, always.
You are my home.

In Jesus' name...

DAY 3

Weary and Burdened
Matthew 11:28-30

Lord, I praise You today.
I bow before You, the Holy One.
You created me. I am Yours.
I lay my weary heart in Your hands.

Lord, I am so tired.
I feel crushed, like I'm in pieces-
fragmented, frantic, and forlorn.
The sadness is stifling.

"Come to Me, all who are weary and heavy-laden,
and I will give you rest."
(11:28)

I come, Jesus, I come.
I run to You, my Lord and Savior.
I am weary, distraught, and burdened.
You know the struggles raging within me.

I come to You, Lord Jesus.
Being with You is my solace.
Crucified and Risen One,
all my hope is in You.

"Take My yoke upon you and learn from Me,
for I am gentle and humble in heart,
and you will find rest for your souls."
(11:29)

I enter Your yoke with You today, Lord Jesus.
I want to learn from You.
Teach me. Reveal Your heart to me.
I want to know You better.

I look not to myself nor to others,
nor to this unreliable and often cruel world,
but I look to You alone as Messiah, Savior,
the One who gives rest to my soul.

"For My yoke is easy and My burden is light."
(11:30)

You are the One who carries the weight.
You are the One who enables and empowers me.
You are the One who loves me
with an everlasting love.
You are the One.

I enter Your work with You, Jesus.
Work Your will in me and through me.
Cause me to rest fully - ever more fully - in You.
I release all burdens to You.

Emotions, thoughts, motives,
fears, worries, concerns, health,
family, friends, relationships, finances.
I entrust all to You.
I praise You, O Holy One.

In Jesus' name...

DAY 4

I Wish I Could Really See
Colossians 1:15-18

Lord, I know that You are near.
Perfect Father, I know that You are ever-present
and always with me.
I know this, but You feel so distant.
I wish I could see You.
I know this is a walk of faith and not sight,
but sometimes I wish I could see - really see.
Open my eyes, Lord. Open my eyes.

The Son is the image of the invisible God,
the firstborn over all creation.
For in him all things were created:
things in heaven and on earth, visible and invisible,
whether thrones or powers or rulers or authorities;
all things have been created through him and for him.
(1:15-16)

Father, I so quickly forget that
You made Yourself visible

in Your Son, Jesus, who came and lived among us.
I do not see You now, Jesus, but I believe in You,
amazing Son of God, Creator of the universe.
You created everything, visible and invisible.
Everything that is owes its existence to You.
You are the reason behind all things,
for all things, including me, were
created by You and for You.

Your power is infinite and unfathomable.
Your wisdom is limitless, and all knowledge is Yours.
You are so far beyond all that is created,
for You are the Uncreated One,
the Forever-Existing One.
You are without beginning, without end,
perfect in all Your attributes and character.
You thought of me, wanted me, planned me,
personally created me, and placed me here, now.

He is before all things, and in him
all things hold together.
And he is the head of the body, the church;
he is the beginning and the firstborn
from among the dead,
so that in everything he might have the supremacy.
(1:17-18)

You exert Your power to hold all things together,
and yet You are not taxed in the least with the effort.
You never tire or grow weary.
You never learn or grow.
You have no needs.
You are the one and only Self-Sufficient One.
You, Jesus, are supreme, so far above, so glorious.
Holy, holy, holy are You,
incomprehensible, God Almighty.
And You, O Christ, live in me, and I live in You.
You have done all this, and I am forever Yours.

Raise me above this ash heap, O my Savior.
Raise my thoughts above my circumstances
and fix my mind on You,
You who love me, accept me,
and are always with me - now, today, forever.

I can't handle it, but You can.
I trust You, Jesus.

In Jesus' name...

DAY 5

Grieving and Angry
Psalm 73:21-26, 28

When my heart was grieved
and my spirit embittered,
I was senseless and ignorant;
I was a brute beast before You.
(73:21-22)

I was angry, and sometimes still am.
Bitterness threatened to invade my soul.
I felt as if I was going crazy.
My heart was frozen.
I was paralyzed on the inside.
Pain overwhelmed me.

Yet I am always with You;
You hold me by my right hand.
You guide me with your counsel,
and afterward You will take me into glory.
(73:23-24)

You did not retreat from me.
You did not pull away.
In my agony, I looked, and You were there.
You were always there.
You are with me, and You have me.
You will not let me go.
I will be with You forever.
This pain, this grief, will end.

Whom have I in heaven but you?
And earth has nothing I desire besides you.
My flesh and my heart may fail,
but God is the strength of my heart
and my portion forever.
(73:25-26)

Forgive me, O Lord,
when I raise anything or anyone above You.
You alone are worthy of worship.
You are always what and who I need.
You alone are my strength, my salvation, my life.
You are my inheritance, my future.
Give me eyes to see You amid this present darkness.

But as for me, it is good to be near God.
I have made the Sovereign LORD my refuge;

I will tell of all your deeds.
(73:28)

In Jesus' name…

DAY 6

In the Grip of Fear
John 1:1-5

Lord, I lift my eyes to You,
Almighty One, Loving Creator.
You are life.
You are my life.

I wonder, Lord. I doubt.
Fear grips and hijacks me.
Grief permeates my being,
and oozes out all over my life.

Lift my eyes, Lord,
to You, to heaven,
to things beyond me and my situation,
beyond these seemingly impossible circumstances.

In the beginning was the Word,
and the Word was with God,
and the Word was God.
He was with God in the beginning.
(1:1-2)

I praise You, Jesus, the Word.
You have always been, and You will always be.
You have no beginning, no end.
You are forever You - the same.

Through him all things were made;
without him nothing was made that has been made.
(1:3)

All that has ever been and will ever be
was created by You, for You, and through You.
You sustain all things, including me.
I was created by You, for You, and through You.

In Him was life,
and that life was the light of all mankind.
(1:4)

Jesus, life was and is in You.
You are life - real life, forever life, eternal life.
You are the light amid the darkness,
shining continually for all, for me.

The light shines in the darkness,
and the darkness has not overcome it.
(1:5)

The darkness continues,
but it has an expiration date.
Darkness could not, cannot conquer You, Jesus.
You are the light. You are life.

In this present darkness, You shine.
In this world of death, You are life.
In my life of turmoil, You bring light and life.
You have overcome, and I am in You.

All praise be to You, Jesus.
I release all to You.

In Jesus' name...

DAY 7

Sad and Discouraged
Ephesians 2:4-10

O Lord, I look to You today.
I wake and I am immediately sad,
forlorn, discouraged.
I am so tired. Please speak to me.
Remind me who I am and why I'm here.

But because of his great love for us,
God, who is rich in mercy,
made us alive with Christ even when
we were dead in transgressions—
it is by grace you have been saved.
(2:4-5)

You love me. Your love is great,
infinite, measureless, eternal.
You had mercy on me, pursuing me, inviting me,
leading me to discover You and to seek You.
I was dead in sin. You made me alive.
You created in me a new person. I was born again.
You saved me, by grace - Your unmerited favor.

I am alive now in Christ, all because of You.
No matter what else happens, this is true.

And God raised us up with Christ and seated us
with him in the heavenly realms in Christ Jesus,
in order that in the coming ages he might show
the incomparable riches of his grace,
expressed in his kindness to us in Christ Jesus.
(2:6-7)

I am alive in Christ. I am in You, Jesus -
raised with You, seated with You
in the heavenly places,
even as I am here, now, amid all
this grief and suffering.
You have a grand and glorious future for me
that is far beyond anything I can conceive or imagine.
You will continue to pour out Your love and
goodness on me forever and ever, without end.
I do not yet feel all this, but I
receive it as truth, by faith.

For it is by grace you have been saved, through faith—
and this is not from yourselves, it is the gift of God—
not by works, so that no one can boast.
(2:8-9)

I could do nothing to contribute anything to this.
I was dead. What can a dead person do?
You did it all, from beginning to end.
All I did was say yes to You, Jesus.
Saved by grace, grace, grace -
unearnable, unmerited favor from You.
Saved through faith - I trusted You and received.
My salvation is a gift from You.

For we are God's handiwork,
created in Christ Jesus to do good works,
which God prepared in advance for us to do.
(2:10)

Jesus, You now live in me,
and You want to live through me.
I yield to You, Lord. Live through me today.
You have things prepared for me to do.
You yourself are my meaning and purpose -
to know You, trust You, love You, and follow You,
whatever might happen.
I am Yours. You made me. You came for me.
You died for me. You conquered sin and death for me.

I surrender myself to You - my thoughts,
my feelings, my will, my worries, my
fears, my future, my relationships.

All of me.

I am Yours.

Empower me to trust in You, and to rest.

In Jesus' name...

DAY 8

My Heart Trembles
Proverbs 12:25, Psalm 94:18-19

Anxiety weighs down the heart,
but a kind word cheers it up.
(Proverbs 12:25)

O Lord, anxiety does indeed weigh upon me.
My heart trembles,
wondering what might happen next,
dreading what else might come.

I am stuck in my own thoughts, Lord.
My mind spins.
Anxious thoughts consume me at times.
Have mercy on me, O God.

I need kind words from You,
my Creator and Redeemer.
Kind words from others would be nice too.

When I said, "My foot is slipping,"
your unfailing love, Lord, supported me.

When anxiety was great within me,
your consolation brought me joy.
(Psalm 94:18-19)

I can look back and see your deliverance
many times in my life.
You are faithful. You are loving.
My circumstances have changed,
but You, O Lord, have not.

My foot is again slipping, O Lord.
I am off balance and fear I will fall.
Once again, support me with Your unfailing love.
Remind me that You will never leave.

Anxiety is once again great within me.
I confess that it hijacks me,
and threatens to control me.
I can barely think, O Lord.

I will cease to fight this anxiety.
I will cease trying to run from it.
By Your grace, I will accept it as it is,
and let You deal with it.

When I said, "My foot is slipping,"
your unfailing love, Lord, supported me.

When anxiety was great within me,
your consolation brought me joy.
(Psalm 94:18-19)

I give this anxiety to You,
and let it pass on through.
Calm me, O my Savior.
Let Your peace rule my anxious heart.

My eyes are on You.
You know it all. You know me.
You are enough, always enough.
Today is Yours. I am Yours.

In Jesus' name...

DAY 9

It Feels Dark Here
John 8:12

Heavenly Father, Lord of the universe,
blessed are You, Sovereign King.
I bow before You, Almighty One,
I receive from You life and love this day.

I try to focus on You, Lord,
but my wavering, scattered brain wanders.
The grief within me churns.
One emotion climbs over another in
a frantic attempt to escape.

Help me, O Father.
Have mercy on me, today.

"I am the light of the world.
Whoever follows me will never walk in darkness,
but will have the light of life."

It feels dark here, Lord Jesus.
Yet You are the light.

You are always shining,
and darkness flees before the light.

I am Yours, Jesus.
I follow You, though not as I ought.
I trust You, but very imperfectly.
Keep me following You, empower me.

"I am the light of the world.
Whoever follows me will never walk in darkness,
but will have the light of life."

I just realized this is not a command,
but rather a promise.
If I follow You,
I will not walk in darkness.

Things may feel dark indeed,
but I do not live in that darkness.
I live in You, the light.
I walk in the light, not in the darkness.

"I am the light of the world.
Whoever follows me will never walk in darkness,
but will have the light of life."

Not only will I never walk in darkness,
but I have You - the light of life.

You, Jesus, live in me -
Savior, Lord, eternal life, light of the world.

I may think and feel many things.
I give all thoughts and emotions to You.
You know them all, You know me.
Shine in and through me today.

You are the light of the world, Jesus.
I follow You.
I will never walk in darkness.
I have You, the light of life.

"I am the light of the world.
Whoever follows me will never walk in darkness,
but will have the light of life."

In Jesus' name...

DAY 10

Strengthen Me
Ephesians 3:14-21

Father in heaven, You are holy,
righteous, merciful, and loving.
Here I am, Lord, my Creator.
I sit in Your presence and wait upon You.
I want to know You better. I need to know You better.

In his letter, Paul prayed for the Ephesians.
I love this prayer, O Lord, and I like to think
that someone might be praying this prayer for me.
I pray this for myself and others today.

For this reason, I kneel before the Father,
from whom every family in heaven
and on earth derives its name.
I pray that out of his glorious riches
he may strengthen you
with power through his Spirit in your inner being,
so that Christ may dwell in your hearts through faith.
(3:14-17)

I fall before You, Lord, my Perfect Father.
Strengthen me today with Your power.
Your resources are infinite because You are infinite.
Your Spirit lives in me, in my inmost being.
O Christ, dwell in me, take up residence,
and make my heart Your home.
Indeed, You have done this,
and I am in awe and thankful.

And I pray that you, being rooted and established in love,
may have power, together with all the Lord's holy people,
to grasp how wide and long and high
and deep is the love of Christ,
and to know this love that surpasses knowledge—
that you may be filled to the measure
of all the fullness of God.
(3:17-19)

No matter what happens or what I feel,
I am planted, rooted, and forever
established in Your love.
O Lord, empower me to grasp the ungraspable -
Your infinite, limitless, and perfect love for me.
Enable me to know - experience - this love
that no human can ever fully understand or fathom.
I cast my fears, worries, hurts, grief, and pain
into the measureless ocean of Your faithful love.

Now to him who is able to do immeasurably
more than all we ask or imagine,

according to his power that is at work within us,

to him be glory in the church and in Christ
Jesus throughout all generations,

for ever and ever! Amen.

(3:20-21)

I ask what seems like the impossible,

but for You it is nothing at all, Infinite, Holy One.

I believe and trust so that I might
begin to understand,

so that I might know and experience
Your love, O Christ.

That I might know and walk with You,

following You on this way of the cross,

yielding myself, my heart, my soul, my mind to You.

I rest in You today.

In Jesus' name...

DAY 11

My Heart is in Danger
Psalm 31:1-5, 7

In you, LORD, I have taken refuge;
let me never be put to shame;
deliver me in your righteousness.
Turn your ear to me, come quickly to my rescue;
be my rock of refuge, a strong fortress to save me.
(31:1-2)

My heart is in danger, O God.
My soul is under attack.
The world is not friendly to my suffering.
Some of those closest to me have turned away.
Feelings of rejection and loneliness stalk me.
There are times when the darkness
closes in around me,
and I cannot see.
I am shattered on the inside.
I hide myself in You.

Since you are my rock and my fortress,
for the sake of your name lead and guide me.

Keep me free from the trap that is set for me,
for you are my refuge.
(31:3-4)

Do not let me go into despair.
Do not let me be tricked and goaded into bitterness.
Do not let these heart wounds consume me.
You know my scars.
You know me.
I am in Your heart.
I am Yours.
Protect and strengthen me, O my God.

Into your hands I commit my spirit;
deliver me, LORD, my faithful God.
I will be glad and rejoice in your love,
for you saw my affliction
and knew the anguish of my soul.
(31:5, 7)

I yield myself to You - all of me.
I choose You over all else and all others.
You see me. You know me.
You hear my heart.
I entrust to You my body,
my mind, my emotions, my will,
my health, my possessions, my relationships,

my family, my reputation, my hopes,
my future, my spirit.
I am Yours - all Yours.
And You are mine.

In Jesus' name...

DAY 12

Too Much Heartache
Isaiah 41:13

I praise You, Creator of all things,
You who hold all things together.
You created me. You provide for me.
Your love and care are infinite.

Lord, I confess that my eyes are weary,
as if I have seen too much.
Too much loss, pain, and suffering.
Too much grief, heartache, and death.

My heart sags within me.
Day after day I am burdened
by persistent, relentless fears and terrors
that chisel away at my soul and body.

For I am the LORD your God
who takes hold of your right hand
and says to you, Do not fear;
I will help you.

Help me, my Father, help me.
I feel lost and adrift.
I feel as if I'm being torn into pieces.
I wonder how much of me is left.
Help me, Jesus, help me.

For I am the LORD your God
who takes hold of your right hand
and says to you, Do not fear;
I will help you.

Lift me up, O King.
Heal my heart, O Savior.
Hold me, for I have no strength.
Let me feel Your strong grip, O Mighty One.
Help me, my Father, my perfect Father,
Help me.

For I am the LORD your God
who takes hold of your right hand
and says to you, Do not fear;
I will help you.

In Jesus' name...

DAY 13

I Don't Feel at Home Here
Philippians 2:20-21

Holy Father, King and Lord of all,
Creator of the universe, my Maker,
I praise and worship You.
I give You thanks, for You are good
and Your love endures forever.

I am weary of this world and this life, O God.
I worry about myself, for I don't
feel at home here anymore.
It's as if the world has nothing to offer me.
Everything has changed. The luster is gone.

But our citizenship is in heaven.
(2:20)

You remind me that this place is
not my ultimate home.
My citizenship is elsewhere, with You, in heaven.
You gave me this citizenship, which will never expire,

through Your Son, Jesus Christ, who died for me
and conquered death to purchase this citizenship.
Now, praise You, I have all the rights and privileges
associated with being a citizen of heaven.
One day, all this suffering and pain will end.

But our citizenship is in heaven.
And we eagerly await a Savior from there,
the Lord Jesus Christ...
(2:20)

Lord Jesus, You are coming.
You are preparing a place for me,
and You will come back to get me,
so that I might be with You, forever.
I will then be free from these wounds
of grief, pain, and suffering.
I will be free to fully experience
You, Your love, Your peace.
I was made for You, to be with You, to dwell with You.
Lord Jesus, I eagerly wait for You.

But our citizenship is in heaven.
And we eagerly await a Savior from
there, the Lord Jesus Christ
who, by the power that enables him to
bring everything under his control,

will transform our lowly bodies so that
they will be like his glorious body.
(2:20-21)

Praise You that I will get a new body, a gift from You.
A body that will never know illness,
weakness, suffering, or death.
I will be made like You, Jesus-
conformed to Your image, Your glorious body.
You will do all this, for You alone can.
You have promised, and You are faithful.
This is certain because You are certain.

No wonder I feel less and less at home here.
No wonder the world is less and less alluring.
Take this broken heart, Lord Jesus.
I am Yours. I surrender myself to You,
as I wait.
In the waiting, give me strength.
Make me faithful, patient, enduring.

In Jesus' name...

DAY 14

I Wish the World Was Different
Deuteronomy 31:8

O Lord, I worship You, Creator of the universe.
You give life to all that exists.
You bless us with good things.
I praise You.

I wake again to a world I wish were different.
I would wish for less turmoil, less suffering, less pain.
The road before me is unknown and appears dark.
I need Your strength and wisdom for
each and every step today.

"The LORD himself goes before
you and will be with you;
He will never leave you nor forsake you."

You are here, O Lord; You are with me.
You go before me; You surround me.
You are faithful; You will never, ever leave me.
You will never cast me off, never abandon me.

Whatever is ahead, whatever is on this road,
You walk with me; You empower my steps.
You are my constant, continual companion.
Cause me to rest, to trust in You.

*"The LORD himself goes before
you and will be with you;
He will never leave you nor forsake you.
Do not be afraid; do not be discouraged."*

You Yourself go before me and are with me.
You are the Creator of all, Lord
of lords, King of kings-
All-powerful, All-knowing, Ever-present.
There is no one like You, Majesty of heaven.

You, Jesus Messiah, have given me eternal life.
You Yourself live in me, never to depart.
Your Holy Spirit dwells in me.
You guide, teach, comfort, and counsel me.

Even with all this, fear knocks at my soul
and threatens my heart, my peace.
Rather than fighting the fear, I give it to You,
and I will keep giving it to You,
fear after fear, worry after worry.
Let Your peace dwell in me and expand,

capturing and permeating my heart more and more,
moment by moment, day by day.

"The LORD himself goes before
you and will be with you;
He will never leave you nor forsake you.
Do not be afraid; do not be discouraged."

Here are my fears, Lord.
I surrender them.
Here are my worries and concerns.
I surrender them.
I surrender volatile emotions and discouragement.
I cling to You, my Lord, Jesus.

In Jesus' name...

DAY 15

I Wake Up to Battle
John 10:11-15

I praise You, Lord of the universe,
Creator of all things.
You are enthroned above all.
Holy, holy, holy are You.
I worship You, Lord of all lords.
You are my Savior, my Shepherd.
Lead me, teach me, provide for and protect me.

"I am the good shepherd.
The good shepherd lays down his life for the sheep."
(10:11)

Amid this pain, I look to You, to the cross,
where You suffered and died for me.
You are good, and what You do is good.
Your goodness is beyond fathoming, limitless, infinite.
I confess my mind cannot grasp the
immensity of your goodness,
nor do I always have eyes to perceive it.

Empower my heart to trust You and rest in You,
in all Your work and sacrifice for me, Good Shepherd.

*The hired hand is not the shepherd
and does not own the sheep.*
*So when he sees the wolf coming, he
abandons the sheep and runs away.*
Then the wolf attacks the flock and scatters it.
*The man runs away because he is a hired
hand and cares nothing for the sheep.*
(10:12-13)

You remind me, my Savior, that I am at war,
that every day I wake up to battle
being waged around and in me.
I praise You that You are already victorious,
even though I have yet to fully experience that.
It feels as though things are falling apart—
as though evil, pain, and suffering are winning.
Yet You remind me that things
are not what they appear,
and that grief, suffering, and evil
have an expiration date.

I know that not everyone will care for and support me,
and certainly not in the ways I would like.
And yet I insanely keep expecting it to be so—
to be treated with kindness, love, and respect

by people and places who do not have
good track records of compassion.

Jesus, You have invested Yourself in me,

not because I deserved it, but because You love me.

In this world of relational dysfunction and disaster,

Empower me to trust and abide in You.

*"I am the good shepherd; I know my
sheep and my sheep know me—*

just as the Father knows me and I know the Father—

and I lay down my life for the sheep.

(10:14-15)

Your love is not based on circumstances or situations.

Your love is beyond both - infinite,
measureless, eternal.

You know me, Jesus, my Shepherd,

and I know You.

I give You myself and all that I carry.

I pour my soul out to You.

Good Shepherd, Savior, Lover of my soul.

In Jesus' name...

DAY 16

I'm Barely Here
Psalm 31:9-12, 14-16

Be merciful to me, Lord, for I am in distress;
my eyes grow weak with sorrow,
my soul and body with grief.
My life is consumed by anguish
and my years by groaning;
my strength fails because of my affliction,
and my bones grow weak.
(31:9-10)

Sometimes, I feel like I'm barely here.
I am existing rather than living.
As if I am watching myself fade away,
slowly disappearing, like a morning mist.
My grief grinds my heart into dust
and shreds my soul into pieces.
Your mercy is my hope,
for only You can hold me together.

Because of all my enemies,
I am the utter contempt of my neighbors

and an object of dread to my closest friends—
those who see me on the street flee from me.
I am forgotten as though I were dead;
I have become like broken pottery.
(31:11-12)

My world has been upended,
and all my relationships are changing.
I am stunned by the world's unfeeling cruelty,
and how mean strangers and even friends can be.
I have been disappointed and dismayed
at the utter lack of compassion and caring.
Even common respect is gone.

My wounds have no value to them.
I am a bother, a nuisance,
and perhaps a reminder of their own pain.
I feel like a shadow,
something less than real and substantial.
Who am I now?
Where do I belong?

But I trust in you, LORD;
I say, "You are my God."
My times are in your hands;
deliver me from the hands of my enemies,
from those who pursue me.

Let your face shine on your servant;
save me in your unfailing love.
(31:14-16)

In Jesus' name...

DAY 17

Weary from Sorrow
John 10:25-26, 40-44

Lord, You are the Alpha and the Omega,
The first and the last, the beginning and the end.
You have always been, and You will always be—
forever unchanging and immutable.
I praise You, O Lord of hosts.

My eyes are weary from sorrow,
from exposure to loss, pain, and evil.
My body is drained and heavy.
My mind is sluggish and distracted.
I feel like I'm not really living, but just existing,
going through the motions of the days—
empty, numb, and exhausted.

Jesus said to her, "I am the resurrection and the life.
The one who believes in me will
live, even though they die;
and whoever lives by believing in me will never die.
Do you believe this?"

(10:25-26)

Yes, I believe this.

No matter how I feel, You are the
resurrection and the life.

No matter what anyone says or does, You
are the resurrection and the life.

No matter what happens, You are
the resurrection and the life.

I believe in You; I trust You.

Even if I die, I will live;

Or if I live until You appear, then I will never die.

Either way, my destination is You.

My destination is life, for You are life.

*Then Jesus said, "Did I not tell you that if you
believe, you will see the glory of God?"*

*So they took away the stone. Then
Jesus looked up and said,*

"Father, I thank you that you have heard me.

*I knew that you always hear me, but I said this
for the benefit of the people standing here,*

that they may believe that you sent me."

*When he had said this, Jesus called in a
loud voice, "Lazarus, come out!"*

*The dead man came out, his hands and
feet wrapped with strips of linen,*

and a cloth around his face.

*Jesus said to them, "Take off the grave
clothes and let him go."*
(10:40-44)

I can only imagine what the people thought,
and how they reacted to all this -
death conquered right before their very eyes.
You are life.
Death must bow before You.
Hallelujah to You, Jesus.

Jesus, You live in me.
Though alive in You, grave clothes still cling to me.
I have thoughts, attitudes, words, and
actions that do not reflect You.
Past failures, wounds, and rejections still haunt me-
offenses that I can't seem to release.

Lazarus was bound and could not deal
with his own grave clothes.
Lord, who can help remove my grave clothes,
so that I can walk with You in freedom and peace?
Surround me with people who love You-
merciful, loving souls You can use in my life
to bring hope, comfort, and healing.
Ultimately, it is You setting me free and
dealing with my grave clothes.

I am free, and yet you are setting
me free, one day at a time.

You are the resurrection and the life, no matter what.
I believe. I trust in You.

In Jesus' name...

DAY 18

I Have Nothing Left
Colossians 3:12-15

Thank you, O God, that I am always with You.
You are ever-present and ever-loving.
You are merciful, compassionate, and gracious.
You hold me up amid these trials and hardships.

I have no self-strength, my Father.
I am spent and feel I have nothing left.
I sit before You, waiting for You, my Savior,
and yet growing weary in the waiting.

Therefore, as God's chosen people, holy and dearly loved,
clothe yourselves with compassion, kindness, humility,
gentleness and patience.
(3:12)

At first, I laugh at these words, O Lord.
They must be for someone else who is not where I am,
but rather for someone with energy and strength-
someone who is not in a season of suffering and pain.

Yet, Jesus, You were thinking of others
as You hung on the cross.

You poured out Your love amid Your
suffering - indeed through it.

You live in me, loving, all-powerful Savior.

Live through me as You wish.

I receive the identity You have given me.

I am one of Your chosen people.

You have cleaned me and made me holy.

I am dearly loved - completely,
perfectly, now and forever.

I put on these spiritual clothes that
You have provided for me.

Jesus, I clothe myself with You today –

Your compassion, Your kindness, Your humility,

Your gentleness, Your patience.

With You, all things are possible.

Bear with each other and forgive one another
if any of you has a grievance against someone.
Forgive as the Lord forgave you.
(3:13)

Empower me, Jesus, to release these extra weights,
and to forgive all offenses and wrongs.

I choose to forgive even with swirling emotions,
in the name of Jesus, the Great Forgiver.

And over all these virtues put on love,
which binds them all together in perfect unity.
(3:14)

I put on love today - Your love -
love that seeks the best of others,
in the power of Christ.
Love others through me, Lord Jesus.
I choose to see the people around me today.

Let the peace of Christ rule in your hearts,
since as members of one body you were called to peace.
And be thankful.
(3:15)

Though I am lonely, I am not alone.
You are with me, and I am a part
of Your forever family.
I choose to let Your peace rule my heart this day,
by Your strength and power.
Grant me a thankful heart, O Lord.
Thank you. Thank you. Thank you.

In Jesus' name...

DAY 19

Tired of Pain
Psalm 42:1-5

As the deer pants for streams of water,
so my soul pants for you, my God.
My soul thirsts for God, for the living God.
When can I go and meet with God?
(42:1-2)

I need You so badly, O Lord.
I need Your presence, Your strength, Your comfort.
I need Your love, Your peace, Your patience.
I need Your power, Your mercy, Your healing.
I need You.

My tears have been my food day and night,
while people say to me all day long,
"Where is your God?"
(42:3)

I too wonder where You are at times, O Lord.
I know the answers. I know You are with me.

I want to experience Your presence,
stronger and stronger each day.

Thank you for the people around me
who love me and bring comfort.
They are blessings from You.
When human comforters are not available,
I will not despair, for You are always here.

These things I remember as I pour out my soul:
how I used to go to the house of God
under the protection of the Mighty One
with shouts of joy and praise
among the festive throng.
(42:3-4)

I look back and weep.
It seems like the former days always
seem better somehow.
I am tired of pain, exhausted by this grueling grief.
Help me to look back and see You-
Your blessings, Your provision, Your love.
Then help me look ahead and know
that You are the same.

Why, my soul, are you downcast?
Why so disturbed within me?

Put your hope in God,
for I will yet praise him,
my Savior and my God.
(42:5)

Be calm, O my soul.
My hope is in You, Lord.
I will praise You today.
I will give thanks to You.

In Jesus' name...

DAY 20

Fearful and Traumatized
James 1:2-5

Perfect Father, Creator of the universe, my Maker.
I come to You again, hurting, wounded, grieving,
wondering how I am going to
make it through this day,
fearful of what awaits me, and traumatized
by all that has happened.

Consider it pure joy, my brothers and sisters,
whenever you face trials of many kinds...
(1:2)

I don't know what to think about this.
My first thought is, "Ridiculous!"
My next thought is, "I can't. How can I?"
And yet Your voice, Your command
to me for my good is clear.
Lord, give me whatever I need to do this.
Even as I ask, I know I have what
I need for I have You.
Jesus, only You can do this, and You live in me-
You, who for the joy set before You endured the cross.

Consider it pure joy, my brothers and sisters,
whenever you face trials of many kinds,
because you know that the testing of
your faith produces perseverance.
(1:2-3)

This is clearly a decision beyond my emotions.
This is a choice to live higher, looking
at You rather than at myself.
I choose to rejoice in trials today
because You are at work.
You, Jesus, faced trials unimaginable
to me, and I follow You.
You use everything for my good, especially
these painful things that happen.
You are always taking me deeper,
into a closer walk with You.
This is the way of the cross: to die to the life I want,
so that I might live in reality, walking with
You, persevering and overcoming.

Let perseverance finish its work
so that you may be mature and complete,
not lacking anything.
(1:4)

It seems that everything valuable in life is hard.
I want to be mature and complete, Lord.

You have me on this path. You are walking with me.
I do not mature myself. You work in and through me
to produce Your fruit - love, joy, peace, patience -
amid all this turmoil, hardship, and emotional pain.
Rather than exhausting myself fighting this reality,
enable me, O Jesus, to lean into
the grief and difficulty.

If any of you lacks wisdom, you should ask God,
who gives generously to all without finding fault,
and it will be given to you.
(1:5)

Amen, Lord Jesus. I lack wisdom.
You have all wisdom.
I embrace You. Fill me with Yourself, Your Spirit.
I yield to You. Give me Your wisdom.
I praise You, my Creator, Redeemer, Savior, Friend.

In Jesus' name...

DAY 21

Scared and Anxious
1 Peter 5:6-7

Lord, I feel so out of control,
perhaps because I am not in control.
I am scared. Even terrified at times.
Anxiety surges up within me.

I have anxiety attacks,
Perhaps they're panic attacks.
This is awful, Lord. Terrible.
I feel paralyzed.

Remind me to breathe, O God.

I humble myself under Your mighty hand,
that You may lift me up in due time.
I cast all my anxiety on You
because You care for me.

I choose to shift my thoughts
from this anxiety to You.

You are never anxious, never panicked.
You are never worried or fearful.

You are mighty indeed.
All power is Yours.
You know all things.
All knowledge is Yours.
I yield to You.

Help me to trust You.
I throw my anxiety to You.
I cast it off and give it to You.
You love me.
You will take care of me.
I confess my doubt and unbelief.
Increase my faith, O Lord.

I say it again...

*I humble myself under Your mighty hand,
that You may lift me up in due time.
I cast all my anxiety on You
because You care for me.*

In Jesus' name...

DAY 22

My Soul Aches
Isaiah 53:1-6

Lord, I come to you again today,
my heart intact and yet in pieces.
My soul aches.
My body and mind are exhausted.
I pour out my soul and lift my eyes to You.
Set my mind upon You, Jesus.

Who has believed our message
and to whom has the arm of the LORD been revealed?
He grew up before him like a tender shoot,
and like a root out of dry ground.
He had no beauty or majesty to attract us to him,
nothing in his appearance that we should desire him.
He was despised and rejected by mankind,
a man of suffering, and familiar with pain.
Like one from whom people hide their faces
he was despised, and we held him in low esteem.

(53:1-3)

Isaiah prophesied about You, Jesus.

You loved us so much that You took on human flesh.

You, miracles of all miracles, dwelt among us -

humble, unassuming, winsome, good, righteous.

Yet we despised and rejected You.

Suffering? You know it all too well.

Pain? You are very familiar with it.

Surely he took up our pain and bore our suffering,
yet we considered him punished by God,
stricken by him, and afflicted.
[5] But he was pierced for our transgressions,
he was crushed for our iniquities;
the punishment that brought us peace was on him,
and by his wounds we are healed.
(53:4-5)

We did not recognize You.

We failed to see who You were.

The nails of the cross,

the brutality of that execution,

was for me -

my sins, my iniquities, my rebellion.

You took my punishment.

Your suffering means my healing.

We all, like sheep, have gone astray,
each of us has turned to our own way;

and the LORD has laid on him
the iniquity of us all.
(53:6)

O Lord Jesus, who am I to complain of suffering?
You know, Lord. You know.
You are with me, in me. I am in You.
Remind me of the constant
companionship I have with You.

You are at work amid my pain.
You waste nothing.
Suffering Savior, now glorified and exalted,
I trust in You.

In Jesus' name...

DAY 23

My Heart is Troubled
John 14:1-3

Here I am, Lord.
You are here, right here, with me.
I embrace You and Your truth,
even if my feelings are awry and jumbled.
My feelings and my situation do
not change who You are.

Yet I confess that my heart is troubled,
as if my soul is shaking, trembling under the weight
of all that has happened and is happening.
I confess I am quickly discouraged,
frustrated, anxious, and sad.
At times, I cannot seem to move.
Other times, I move but sense I'm going nowhere.

"Do not let your hearts be troubled.
You believe in God; believe also in me.
My Father's house has many rooms;
if that were not so,

would I have told you that I am going
there to prepare a place for you?
And if I go and prepare a place for you,
I will come back and take you to be with
me that you also may be where I am."

You know my heart, Lord Jesus.
You know me. You know it all.
You have a plan for me.
I am on a journey to the Father's house.
I am passing through here on my way to heaven.
Jesus, You Yourself are preparing a place for me.

You are both with me and in me,
even as You prepare a place for me.
I have a destiny which You have
won and secured for me.
My future is to be with You where You are.
You Yourself will come back and take me there.
You have done it all and are doing it all, Lord Jesus.

Today, You are at work in me,
preparing me for that day, that glorious moment,
when I will see You and
when all this pain, grief, and suffering
will be swallowed up
by Your perfect peace, comfort, love, and safety.

I lean into this, my future-
this indescribable gift from You.

In the meantime, empower me to endure.
Deliver, calm, heal, purify, and strengthen me.
Remind me, Jesus. Remind me of what's coming.

"Do not let your hearts be troubled.
You believe in God; believe also in me.
My Father's house has many rooms;
if that were not so,
would I have told you that I am going
there to prepare a place for you?
And if I go and prepare a place for you,
I will come back and take you to be with me
that you also may be where I am."

In Jesus' name...

DAY 24

Am I Going Crazy?
James 5:7-11

Lord, I can barely sit still. I'm nervous, anxious.
My mind is whirling. My emotions are churning.
I fear I'm about to lose it, and this isn't the first time.
Lord, am I going crazy?

Things are so different. The world is changing.
I can't keep up. I don't want to.
I don't like where all this is heading.
I feel like I'm being dragged along against my will
into feelings, thoughts, and places I don't want to be.

Be patient, then, brothers and sisters,
until the Lord's coming.
See how the farmer waits for the land
to yield its valuable crop,
patiently waiting for the autumn and spring rains.
You too, be patient and stand firm,
because the Lord's coming is near.
(5:7-8)

Patience. I don't have it, Lord. But You know this.

Your Spirit is patient, and Your Spirit dwells in me.

You remind me my self-strength is small –

tiny and insufficient -

while Your strength is limitless.

You are all-powerful.

I can't, but You can, and You will.

I yield to You.

Produce Your fruit, Your patience in me, Holy Spirit.

Like the farmer's crop, I trust that growth and life is going on under the surface of this barren wilderness.

Hold me up, Lord.

Enable me to stand, and to stand firm.

I look for You. I wait for You. I long for You.

Don't grumble against one another, brothers and sisters,
or you will be judged. The Judge is standing at the door!
(5:9)

Guard me from this grumbling, O Lord.

I release offenses and hurts. I forgive.

I choose to love. I choose to be patient.

Empower me to live like You might come today,

because You just might.

Brothers and sisters, as an example of
patience in the face of suffering,
take the prophets who spoke in the name of the Lord.

As you know, we count as blessed
those who have persevered.

You have heard of Job's perseverance and have
seen what the Lord finally brought about.

The Lord is full of compassion and mercy.

(5:10-11)

I am in good company, Lord.

The prophets and Job served You,
the same God I serve.

You do not change. You empowered them.

You empower me. Renew my mind, Lord.

Let me see what a privilege it is
to know and serve You.

Let me remember the endgame - Your coming.

Then suffering, grief, and pain will be a memory.

Today, I rest in You, dwelling in
Your compassion and mercy.

In Jesus' name...

DAY 25

Trying and Failing
Psalm 40:1-5

I waited patiently for the LORD;
he turned to me and heard my cry.
He lifted me out of the slimy pit,
out of the mud and mire;
he set my feet on a rock
and gave me a firm place to stand.
(40:1-2)

You have done this for me many times, O Lord.
You have delivered me again and again.
How many times have you rescued me
and I wasn't even aware of it?
I do not know what has not happened -
all that you have protected me from.
You hear my every cry.

He put a new song in my mouth,
a hymn of praise to our God.

Many will see and fear the LORD
and put their trust in him.
(40:3)

In the past, You have enabled me to sing,
even while my heart was broken.
You will strengthen me to sing again.
Shine in me, and shine through me, O Lord.

Blessed is the one
who trusts in the LORD,
who does not look to the proud,
to those who turn aside to false gods.
(40:4)

My idols have been many, Lord.
How numerous are the things and people
I have elevated above You.
Purify my heart to worship You alone,
and to trust You, O God my Savior.
I am tired of trying and failing.
I want to rest in You and trust.

Many, LORD my God,
are the wonders you have done,
the things you planned for us.
None can compare with you;
were I to speak and tell of your deeds,

they would be too many to declare.
(40:5)

I will practice Your presence today, O God.
You are here, now, with me.
You, Almighty God, Creator of all.
You know my tears, my pain, my suffering.
I give it all to You, O Holy One.
I open my heart wide to You.
Bring healing, Lord,
in Your time, in Your way.

In Jesus' name...

DAY 26

Surrounded, Trapped, Outnumbered
2 Kings 6:15-17

*When the servant of the man of God got up
and went out early the next morning,*

*an army with horses and chariots
had surrounded the city.*

"Oh no, my lord! What shall we do?" the servant asked.

(6:15)

O God, similar to this servant,
I feel surrounded, trapped, outnumbered,
as if I'm being relentlessly squeezed.
Sometimes, I find it hard to breathe.

I can feel so small, so alone,
so weak, vulnerable, and helpless.
Perhaps I am indeed all of those, except for alone,
for I know You, Jesus, are with me, in me.

With the servant, my heart cries,
"Oh no, my Lord! What shall I do?"

"Don't be afraid," the prophet answered.
"Those who are with us are more than
those who are with them."
(6:16)

Yes, Lord. I am so quick to forget
the realities of the unseen, spiritual realm.
Every day, every moment, is a spiritual battle
amid a cosmic, spiritual war.
I surrender the fallacy that this is all about me-
that my life is about me,
and that these struggles are about me,
All this is part of a larger picture, a larger story.
Your grand story.

And Elisha prayed, "Open his eyes,
LORD, so that he may see."
Then the LORD opened the servant's eyes,
and he looked and saw the hills
full of horses and chariots of fire all around Elisha.
(6:17)

O Lord, open my eyes.
Give me discernment.
According to Your will for me,
may I be more aware of this battle that is raging.

Most of all, remind me that You are already victorious,
Conquering King of all.
You, Jesus, have conquered sin and death,
and You brought me into Your life.

Open my eyes, O God, that I might see.
Give me Your strength to endure,
to persevere patiently, walking with You,
following You, trusting You.
You are the Victorious One, my
Creator, my Redeemer,
My Savior and my Lord.

In Jesus' name...

DAY 27

Tired of Faking It
Matthew 5:3-6

Lord Jesus, I want to follow You.
I need to follow You.
You alone can lead me through
this wilderness of pain and grief.

My strength is failing.
I am tired of faking it and going through the motions.
I am ashamed of my weakness.
I lay myself before You, O Lord.

"Blessed are the poor in spirit,
for theirs is the kingdom of heaven."
(5:3)

My losses have caved in upon me.
Sometimes I can barely breathe.
I feel shattered.
I grieve and cannot lift my head.

"Blessed are those who mourn,
for they shall be comforted."
(5:4)

The world runs over me, unconcerned.
I feel invisible,
while the powerful flourish
and seem to live without a care.

"Blessed are the gentle,
for they shall inherit the earth."
(5:5)

I sought meaning in empty places-
in things, money, prestige, and reputation.
Chasing after the wind
left me exhausted and empty.

"Blessed are those who hunger and
thirst for righteousness,
for they shall be satisfied."
(5:6)

All my life I was looking for You, but didn't know it.
Jesus, You are life.
You alone can save and satisfy.

This world will only frustrate me.
This is not my home. You are my home.
Be my home, Lord Jesus.

In Jesus' name…

DAY 28

I Have So Many Needs
Philippians 4:12-13, 19-20

I praise You, Lord, my Shepherd.
You are vast, unfathomable, and infinite.
Your resources are limitless and extravagant.
You are the One who meets my needs.

And I have so many needs, Lord.
So many needs.
This grief, pain, and suffering appear endless.
I often feel empty and forlorn.

*I know what it is to be in need, and I
know what it is to have plenty.
I have learned the secret of being content
in any and every situation,
whether well fed or hungry, whether
living in plenty or in want.
I can do all this through him who gives me strength.
(4:12-13)*

Circumstances change. Situations are altered.
I know my life was upended and changed forever.

One loss led to another loss that led to more loss.

As my losses piled up, You were with me in the battle.

You are still with me, in me, working
for me and blessing me,

though I may not know or be able to perceive it.

You are my no-matter-what Savior,
always with me, always in me.

I can do today because You are my strength.

I can do all this through him who gives me strength.
(4:13)

All things. All this.

I can do all this only through You.

It is Your strength, not mine.

It is about You, not about me.

I give today's challenges to You.

I give this sadness, fear, guilt, and anger to You.

I give You this grief, this pain, all this disappointment.

I can do today through You who gives me strength.

And my God will meet all your needs
according to the riches of his glory in Christ Jesus.
(4:19)

All my needs. All of them.

You will meet all my needs from
Your boundless resources.

Your resources are inexhaustible,

and You are extravagantly generous.

I receive this word from You - this promise.

I choose to believe it and to live like I believe it today.

Empower and enable me, Jesus, my Savior and Lord.

I can do today through You, for You are my strength.

To our God and Father be glory for ever and ever. Amen.
(4:20)

Amen and amen.

I can do all things through You.

You can do anything You want through me.

Jesus, fill me.

Fill me so that You might be all and everything to me.

In Jesus' name...

DAY 29

Burdens, Fears, and Worries
Isaiah 53:7-9

Lord, this world seems so full of pain.
Grief and suffering are everywhere.
Within me, burdens, fears, and worries
compete for attention.

I breathe. I pause.
I remember You, Lord.
I think of You, Jesus.

He was oppressed and afflicted,
yet he did not open his mouth;
he was led like a lamb to the slaughter,
and as a sheep before its shearers is silent,
so he did not open his mouth.
(53:7)

You were without sin,
yet hated, condemned,
misunderstood, rejected, reviled.

You did not defend Yourself.
This was Your mission-
to suffer and die for me.

By oppression and judgment he was taken away.
Yet who of his generation protested?
For he was cut off from the land of the living;
for the transgression of my people he was punished.
(53:8)

I look to You, to the cross.
You were judged in my place.
You bore my penalty.
I bow before You, Suffering Savior.
By dying You vanquished my sin.
By rising You conquered death.

He was assigned a grave with the wicked,
and with the rich in his death,
though he had done no violence,
nor was any deceit in his mouth.
(53:9)

I fix my eyes on You, Jesus.
You are my Savior, my leader, my mentor.
I follow You.
Teach me to walk in Your ways

amid the pain and grief of this world
and the challenges of my own heart.

I give myself to You.
I am Yours.
O Christ who lives in me,
Heal, strengthen, and comfort.
Live through me today.

In Jesus' name...

I Don't Feel Like Praying
Matthew 6:9-13

Lord, many times I do not feel like praying.
Then I realize how ridiculous that is.
I must think it takes effort.
In reality, prayer is as natural as breathing.

You are always with me,
and I am always with You.
Our companionship is continual and ongoing.
Yet, I am not aware of You at times.
Prayer is simply becoming aware once again of reality,
and consciously remembering You.

"Pray, then, in this way:
'Our Father who is in heaven,
Hallowed be Your name.
'Your kingdom come.
Your will be done,
On earth as it is in heaven.'"
(6:9-10)

You are my Father, the Perfect Father -
my holy, righteous, and loving Father.
All praise, honor, and glory be to You.
What matters is Your kingdom.
What matters is what You want, Your will.
For all of this is about You.
This is Your story.
Thank you for including me, us,
in Your grand and glorious story.

Lord, bring about Your perfect will,
in Your way, in Your time,
in my battered and broken heart,
and in this battered and broken world.

'Give us this day our daily bread.'
(6:11)

You know what I need today.
All my needs are met already in You, Jesus.
Enable me to walk with You,
to follow and commune with You.
Let me live out of the abundance I have in You.
Apart from You, I can do nothing.

'And forgive us our debts,
as we also have forgiven our debtors.'
(6:12)

I confess all sin to You.
I receive Your forgiveness for all my sin-
Past, present, and future.
O Jesus, empower me to forgive,
and to forgive quickly.
I release all past and present offenses to You.
I lay all wounds and rejections before You.

'And do not lead us into temptation,
but deliver us from the evil one.'
(6:13)

Protect me, O God, from temptation and sin.
Protect me, O Jesus, from the evil one.
Guard my heart, my mind, my body.
Thank you, Father.

In Jesus' name...

DAY 31

Wounds, Memories, Rejections
1 Peter 4:12-14

Lord, You are the Alpha and the Omega.
You are the first and the last, the
beginning and the end.
You are the Creator of all. You
sustain all. You bless all.
Your wisdom, power, and love are
beyond comprehension.

Even with all that has happened,
Your blessings overflow.
You give me life. You love me perfectly.
You have given me hope - certainty
- and a glorious future.
You are my hope, my future, my life.
You have rescued me, Jesus. Rescue me.
Rescue me from these oppressive thoughts and feelings
that drive me places I don't like and don't want to go.
The losses, wounds, and memories
assault me continually.

And then there are the rejections -
abandonments by those I trusted.

I gave my heart, and they broke
it - and continue to shatter it.

It's as if I have become a loathsome creature to them,
like some disease they are desperately trying to avoid.

Dear friends, do not be surprised at the fiery ordeal
that has come on you to test you,
as though something strange were happening to you.
(4:12)

I forget that this is not about me.

I forget that others have been through
such things, and worse.

I stare into the rearview mirror and forget
to look through the windshield.

Yes, this is an ordeal, and You are in the fire with me.

You are sufficient for this fire, this
ordeal - and all ordeals and trials.

You have sustained others in hardship,
and You will sustain me.

Indeed, You are sustaining me.

Fiery ordeals are inevitable. You are always sufficient.

But rejoice inasmuch as you participate
in the sufferings of Christ,
so that you may be overjoyed when his glory is revealed.

If you are insulted because of the name of Christ,
you are blessed, for the Spirit of glory
and of God rests on you.
(4:13-14)

Sometimes I suffer because of what I have done.

Other times I suffer because I live in a
broken world of loss and pain.

Still other times, I suffer because I am Yours,

standing against evil and pointing to You.

Lord, give me joy and peace when
I share in Your sufferings.

Cause me to look forward and rejoice,

knowing that You are coming and
that it could be today.

Fill me, Jesus, for this day, for whatever comes.

You have blessed me with every
spiritual blessing in Christ.

I am blessed, blessed, blessed indeed.

And more blessing is coming, when You appear.

Until then, I rejoice, for You are with me in the fire.

You are always and forever sufficient.

In Jesus' name...

THE SECOND MONTH

DAY 1

Guilt Haunts Me
Psalm 40:11-13, 16-17

Do not withhold your mercy from me, LORD;
may your love and faithfulness always protect me.
For troubles without number surround me;
my sins have overtaken me, and I cannot see.
They are more than the hairs of my head,
and my heart fails within me.
(40:11-12)

Lord, guilt haunts me.
My regrets are piled up to heaven.
Things I wish I had not said and done.
Things I wish I had said and done.
I am badly wounded, yes,
but I have wounded others also.
How many and how much,
You alone know, O God.

Trouble seems to multiply by the day.
My mind is filled with things I cannot fix,

Failures I cannot make amends for.
With You there is forgiveness,
and I confess all this to You.

Be pleased to save me, LORD;
come quickly, LORD, to help me.
(40:13)

Remove my guilt and wash me clean.
Your Son gave His life for me.
He died my death.
He suffered my penalty.

What amazing love.
It is finished. It is done.
And I am rescued and forever free.
I receive your complete and total forgiveness.
I seek You.

May all who seek you rejoice and be glad in you;
may those who long for your saving help always say,
"The LORD is great!"
(40:16)

You are great, O Lord.
Thank you for your forgiveness.
Empower me to forgive as I have been forgiven.

Blessed beyond measure, my heart still aches.

I grieve. I mourn.

I continue to look to You.

As for me, I am poor and needy;
may the LORD think of me.
You are my help and my deliverer;
You are my God, do not delay.
(40:17)

In Jesus' name...

DAY 2

I Feel Anxious Again
Philippians 4:6-7

Lord, I feel anxious again.
In fact, I feel anxious a lot,
Perhaps even all the time.
Peace feels far away at present.
I can hear You saying through Your Word,

"Do not be anxious about anything."
(4:6)

That seems so impossible,
Yet I know that this is a command.
You want me to have peace.
You don't want me to be anxious.
Yet anxiety rages within me.
I can't do this, but I believe You can do it in me.

Align my mind and heart with Your Word:

Do not be anxious about anything,
but in every situation,

by prayer and petition,
with thanksgiving,
present your requests to God.
(4:6)

When I find myself worried,
remind me to pray, to seek, to ask,
and to trust.
Remind me to give thanks,
and leave my requests with You.
As I pray, ask, thank, and trust,
You give me a promise:

And the peace of God,
which transcends all understanding,
will guard your hearts and your minds
in Christ Jesus. (4:7)

Guard my heart and mind, O Lord,
With Your peace,
No matter what external turmoil is brewing.
I follow You, Jesus.
I am in You, safe and secure.
I am Yours.

Do not be anxious about anything,
but in every situation, by prayer and petition,

with thanksgiving, present your requests to God.

And the peace of God, which
transcends all understanding,

will guard your hearts and your minds in Christ Jesus.

(4:6-7)

In Jesus' name…

DAY 3

My Relationships are Changing.
Matthew 7:12-14

Heavenly Father, thank you for life.
Thank you for the air I breathe.
Thank you for the gift of prayer.
Thank you for this day,
another day to walk with You here.

I am feeling my losses today, O Lord.
It feels like my heart is riddled with holes
with a different emotion leaking out of each one,
joining together in this continual cascade of grief.

One loss leads to more loss.
My world and life seem so, so different.
My relationships are changing, Lord,
stretching like an army of rubber bands,
some fraying and threatening to snap.

"In everything, therefore,
treat people the same way you want them to treat you,
for this is the Law and the Prophets."

(7:12)

I cannot control how others respond, can I?
In fact, their response may not be about me,
but rather about them and their own hearts.
By Your grace, O Lord, I can
choose to treat them well,
with respect, love, compassion, and forgiveness.

This is Your way, Jesus,
and I am Your disciple, Your apprentice.
Live through me in all my relationships,
and bring honor to Yourself.
Use me as a pipeline of Your life and love.

"Enter through the narrow gate;
for the gate is wide and the way is
broad that leads to destruction,
and there are many who enter through it."
(7:13)

This is Your way, Jesus, the narrow way,
the road less travelled.
I will swim upstream with You,
trusting You for all that is needed
as You lead on, undeterred.

Keep my feet on Your narrow way
and off the broader path that is far

from hope, healing, and all that is good.

Do not let me follow the crowd.

Fix my gaze on You, Jesus.

"For the gate is small and the way
is narrow that leads to life,
and there are few who find it."
(7:14)

All are invited but so few choose to follow.

You, Jesus, are life.

My needs for love, acceptance, meaning, safety,

peace and purpose are all met in You.

I believe this, though I do not fully experience it yet.

"In everything, therefore,
treat people the same way you want them to treat you,
for this is the Law and the Prophets.
Enter through the narrow gate;
for the gate is wide and the way is
broad that leads to destruction,
and there are many who enter through it.
For the gate is small and the way is
narrow that leads to life,
and there are few who find it."
(7:12-14)

All make their own choice.

My choice is to follow You.

You are my gate, my road, my way, my life.

I am in You, and You are in me.

Fill me and empower me today.

In Jesus' name...

DAY 4

The Pains of My Heart
1 Thessalonians 5:16-18

Abba, Father, I cannot lift my head today,
or perhaps I don't want to.
The pains of my heart are unspeakable.
I am running out of words to describe this agony.
Lord, You know. You know me. You know my misery.
Have mercy, Lord. Be gracious to me.

*Rejoice always, pray continually, give
thanks in all circumstances;
for this is God's will for you in Christ Jesus.*

I hear these words today and anger
is triggered within me.
How can I do this? I cannot. I do not want to.
Then, I sit with these thoughts, these emotions,
and know that in You I can do all
things, Jesus my strength.
I look up, and I will rejoice in You,
in Your presence with me.

You never leave or forsake me.

You live in me, and I live in You.

In this world of death, I have forever life in You.

Rejoice always, pray continually, give
thanks in all circumstances;
for this is God's will for you in Christ Jesus.

Though I have You, I seek You, Jesus,
King of kings, Lord of lords.

Empower me to live a life of prayer,
a life of talking with You,

listening to You, conversing with You, yielding to You.

Do this in and through me, for my
self-strength means nothing.

Lord, make prayer as natural as breathing.

Cause me to practice Your presence continually,

aware of You, walking in Your Spirit, following You,

step by step, moment by moment, hour by hour.

Rejoice always, pray continually, give
thanks in all circumstances;
for this is God's will for you in Christ Jesus.

No matter what has happened or what happens,

I can still give thanks, for You are here, in me.

I have You, Jesus. I have Your life in me - eternal life.

I have your living Word, Your sure
and certain promises.

Turn my heart to see and focus on what
I have rather than what I've lost,

and instill deep within me great gratitude.

Open the eyes of my heart to see
You - to see You at work.

Open my mouth in thanksgiving, in all circumstances.

In my measly self-strength, all this is impossible.

In Your strength all this is more than possible.

Lord Jesus, live through me continually,
as a channel of Your life.

I will rejoice always. I will pray continually.

I will give thanks in all circumstances,
by Your grace and power,

For this is Your will for me.

In Jesus' name...

DAY 5

I Long to Feel Better
Psalm 27:7-14

Hear my voice when I call, LORD;
be merciful to me and answer me.
My heart says of you, "Seek his face!"
Your face, Lord, I will seek.
(27:7-8)

I long for so many things, LORD.
I long for relief, for comfort, for peace.
I long to be loved for who I am.
I long for this season to be over.
I long to feel better, to feel stronger.
Underneath it all, I long for You, my Creator,
for all these needs are ultimately met only in Christ.

Do not hide Your face from me,
do not turn Your servant away in anger;
You have been my helper.
Do not reject me or forsake me,

God my Savior.
Though my father and mother forsake me,
the LORD will receive me.
(27:9-10)

Though other relationships wither,
You are fully committed to me.
I am weak and vulnerable,
but You are my strength.
I declare my complete and utter dependence.
I cling to You, my Lord and my God.

Teach me your way, LORD;
lead me in a straight path
because of my oppressors.
Do not turn me over to the desire of my foes,
for false witnesses rise up against me,
spouting malicious accusations.
(27:11-12)

There is little sympathy and even less empathy
in this self-focused, narcissistic world.
Why do I keep expecting support
from those who can't provide it?
Raise me above the fray, O Lord.
In the heat of the battle
I look to You, O Faithful One.

I remain confident of this:
I will see the goodness of the LORD
in the land of the living.
Wait for the LORD;
be strong and take heart
and wait for the LORD.
(27:13-14)

In Jesus' name...

DAY 6

Weary, Tired, Discouraged
Luke 10:38-42

Lord, I come to You again today,
Weary, tired, and discouraged.
The world is shaking, seemingly tottering
on the brink of disaster and ruin.

My world is shaking too,
Along with my mind and heart.
Nothing seems the same,
I have lost so much and continue to lose more.

*Now as they were traveling along, Jesus entered a village;
and a woman named Martha
welcomed Him into her home.*
(10:38)

Lord Jesus, like Martha, I welcome You.
Make my heart Your home,
And abide in me and empower me to abide in You.
You are my home. Be my home, Jesus.

*Martha had a sister called Mary, who
was seated at the Lord's feet,
listening to His word. (10:39).*

Lord Jesus, like Mary, I humble myself.
I sit at Your feet today, now, in this moment.
Give me ears to hear and a heart to understand
as I listen to Your word.

*But Martha was distracted with all her
preparations; and she came up to Him and said,*

*"Lord, do You not care that my sister has left me to
do all the serving alone? Then tell her to help me."*

But the Lord answered and said to her,

*"Martha, Martha, you are worried and bothered about
so many things; but only one thing is necessary,*

*for Mary has chosen the good part,
which shall not be taken away from her."*

(10:40-42)

I confess, Lord, that I too am
distracted by many things,

some of which are important,
while some do not matter.

I get frustrated that others do not
do what they should,

or what I think they should.

I worry. A lot. All the time, in fact.
Like Martha, so many things bother me.
I am frayed and frazzled trying to keep up
while grief and pain gnaw away at me.

"But only one thing is necessary,
for Mary has chosen the good part,
which shall not be taken away from her."
(10:42)

One thing. You.
Sitting at Your feet.
Listening to You.
Making You my home.
Listening.
Learning to rest and to trust.
Yes, only one thing is necessary.

O Jesus, fill me.
Live in me, live through me.
I look to You,
my one necessary thing.

In Jesus' name…

DAY 7

Merely Existing
1 Peter 1:13, 17

All praise be to You, Creator of the universe,
Hope of the world, my Perfect Father, my God.
You are worthy of all praise,
adoration, glory, and thanks.
You are exalted above all.

Lord, at times I wonder if I am really living.
I feel like I'm barely surviving, or even merely existing.
I'm physically alive and going through the motions,
while emotionally numb and mentally exhausted.
You remind me that this is temporary,
that now is not forever, and that things will change.
Yet, I am frightened to look forward
to much of anything.
I no longer feel at home here.

Therefore, with minds that are alert and fully sober,
set your hope on the grace to be brought to you
when Jesus Christ is revealed at his coming.

(1:13)

Yes, Lord. I know You are coming, but when?
I am so weary with waiting, I'm
afraid my hope is slipping,
almost like I'm scared to look up anymore
for fear that I've gotten it wrong somehow.
My heart can't handle any more shattering.
Renew my mind, Jesus. Awaken me.
Move my wandering thoughts to You.
Set my mind on You - and You alone.

When You are revealed, Lord Jesus - when You appear,
I will be transformed and see You as You are.
This vicious, exasperating struggle will be over,
in a flash, in an instant, and I will be with You forever.
Grace - unmerited, unearnable favor from You,
the fullness of my salvation will become reality,
and I will be changed, completely and forever,
to be like You, Lord Jesus, holy and righteous.

Since you call on a Father who judges
each person's work impartially,
live out your time as foreigners here in reverent fear.
(1:17)

Yes, Father. What I do, how I live, is important.
I give my life - all of me and all of this - to You.

I ask You to fill me with Your Spirit,
and to live through me to honor Yourself.
This is not my home. I am a citizen of heaven.
I reside here temporarily, longing for my true place.
Cause me to live out my citizenship well,
loving You and loving others.

Therefore, with minds that are alert and fully sober,
set your hope on the grace to be brought to you
when Jesus Christ is revealed at his coming.
(1:13)

Since you call on a Father who judges
each person's work impartially,
live out your time as foreigners here in reverent fear.
(1:17)

Jesus, You are my home.
All other residences are temporary.
I abide in You today. Let Your words abide in me.
Sustain me. Provide for whatever my needs are today.
I trust You. I rely on You. I love You.

In Jesus' name...

DAY 8

Traveling This Wilderness
Isaiah 53:10-12

I praise You, O King of heaven.
There is none like You.
Your blessings are too many to count.
Amid this grief, I look to You.

Jesus, You are my Leader, my Shepherd,
as I travel through this wilderness.
You know the path.
You are the way.

Yet it was the LORD's will to crush
him and cause him to suffer,
and though the LORD makes his life an offering for sin,
he will see his offspring and prolong his days,
and the will of the LORD will prosper in his hand.
After he has suffered,
he will see the light of life and be satisfied;
by his knowledge my righteous servant will justify many,
and he will bear their iniquities.

(53:10-11)

Even as You suffered, Jesus,
the promise of victory was sure.
Your triumph was certain.
O Christ, You are alive forever.

You have taken away my sin,
and brought me into Yourself and into life.
Suffering Servant, Conqueror of death, Savior, Lord.
I am one of Your offspring.
I am Yours.
I rest in You.

Therefore I will give him a portion among the great,
and he will divide the spoils with the strong,
because he poured out his life unto death,
and was numbered with the transgressors.
For he bore the sin of many,
and made intercession for the transgressors.
(53:12)

You invite me to walk with You today.
You are at work in me
to make me more like Yourself.
This is my purpose, my mission,
to become more and more like You.

Here I am.

I give You myself, this pain, this grief,

these trials and difficulties.

They are too much for me,

but You carry them - and me - with ease.

Be honored and praised today,

Lord Jesus.

In Jesus' name...

DAY 9

Deliverance from Fear
Psalm 34:4

O Lord, my heart is troubled.
My mind is disturbed.
Fear and grief plague and assail me,
threatening to dismantle and undo me.

I look to You, Jesus my Savior.
I look to You for strength and help.
You are my rock, my fortress,
Lord of the universe, my loving God.

I sought the LORD, and He answered me;
He delivered me from all my fears.

I seek You, Lord Jesus.
You alone can save, deliver, and help.
The help of mere mortals is useless.
And my own strength amounts to less than nothing.

I present myself to You, Jesus.

I am Yours, and You are mine.

I live in You, and You live in me.

I choose to trust You.

I sought the LORD, and He answered me;

He delivered me from all my fears.

I will listen to You, Lord Jesus.

My eyes are on You, my Savior.

My heart, mind, soul, and body are Yours.

Lord of grace, mercy, and love, I worship You.

I look to You - You alone.

You are my Deliverer.

You have delivered me and will deliver me.

My trust is in You, my Jesus.

I sought the LORD, and He answered me;

He delivered me from all my fears.

Jesus, loving Conqueror of sin and death,

You have conquered my fears.

Though I do not yet feel this, it will be so,

in Your time, in Your way.

I trust in You.

I sought the LORD, and He answered me;
He delivered me from all my fears.

In Jesus' name...

DAY 10

I Struggle and Wince
Psalm 86:1-7, 10-12

Hear me, LORD, and answer me,
for I am poor and needy.
Guard my life, for I am faithful to you;
save your servant who trusts in you.
You are my God;
have mercy on me, Lord,
for I call to you all day long.
(86:1-3)

Open my heart to You, O Lord.
Enable me to be honest with you,
hiding nothing, sharing everything.
For You know it all, O my God,
all that lurks deep within me,
My wounds, my complaints,
my grief and suffering.

I am poor in spirit and desperately needy.
I am dependent on You for all, everything.

I struggle to yield.

I wince at full surrender,

reluctant to trust for fear of being hurt yet again.

In my doubt, I choose to cling to You.

I choose to trust You,

though You know my trust is far from complete.

You embrace me.

You know all my shortcomings.

Bring joy to your servant, LORD,

for I put my trust in you.

You, LORD, are forgiving and good,

abounding in love to all who call to you.

(86:4-5)

Enable me to receive Your love.

Empower me to know the limitless love of Christ.

I choose to believe, that one day I might understand,

instead of fighting to understand that I might believe.

I choose to trust,

for running from You is futile,

and fighting against You has crushed me.

Because of Your great love,

You relentlessly pursue me.

Thank you, Jesus.

Hear my prayer, LORD;
listen to my cry for mercy.
When I am in distress, I call to you,
because you answer me.
(86:6-7)

Though at times I do not hear or perceive it,
You always answer my soul's cries.
You always offer Yourself as the answer
to all my needs, pains, and afflictions.
You want me. You created me to want You.
O Lord, help me to yield.
Pry open my clenched fists,
that I might receive from You all You have for me.

For you are great and do marvelous deeds;
you alone are God.
Teach me your way, LORD,
that I may rely on your faithfulness;
give me an undivided heart,
that I may fear your name.
I will praise you, Lord my God, with all my heart;
I will glorify your name forever.
(86:10-12)

In Jesus' name...

DAY 11

This Relentless Storm
John 6:16-21

When evening came, His disciples went down to the lake,
where they got into a boat and set off
across the lake for Capernaum.
By now it was dark, and Jesus had not yet joined them.
A strong wind was blowing and the waters grew rough.
(6:16-18)

Lord, a strong wind is blowing.
The waters around me are growing rough.
Though I have been in storms before,
this one shows no signs of relenting.
As the intensity of this storm increases,
I confess that I feel distant from You at times,
almost as if You are not present,
as if I am alone amid the waves.

When they had rowed about three or four miles,
they saw Jesus approaching the boat,
walking on the water; and they were frightened.

But he said to them, "It is I; don't be afraid."
(6:19-20)

I am exhausted from battling this storm, Lord.
The constant rowing against the
storm has exhausted me.
My strength is gone, my resilience is fading.
My grip on the oars is slipping.
I am scared. Terrified. I feel so alone.
I read the words, "It is I; don't be afraid."

I stare into the storm, soaked and shivering.

"It is I; don't be afraid."
(6:20)

You are with me in this storm.
You are here, with me, now, in this moment.
You are not only with me, Jesus,
But You are in me, and I am in You.

"It is I; don't be afraid."
(6:20)

Help me to breathe, Lord Jesus.
Empower me to fix my eyes not on the storm,
but on You, Lord of creation, Lord of all storms.

But he said to them, "It is I; don't be afraid."
Then they were willing to take him into the boat,
and immediately the boat reached the shore
where they were heading. (John 16:20-21)

O Lord Jesus, come into my boat.
I receive You and all You have for me.
You are at work in me, and You will
finish and complete Your work.
You know where all this is heading.
Renew my mind and enable me to follow You,
amid this storm and all storms.
You are my Shepherd, my Savior, my Guide, my Lord.
I cling to You and Your Word.

"It is I; don't be afraid."
(6:20)

In Jesus' name...

DAY 12

I Can Barely Think
Hebrews 12:1-3

I praise You, Father, Son, Holy Spirit.
You are my life, my strength, my all and everything.
I am so weary, Lord. My body
aches, revealing my heart.
I can barely think. Speak to me, my Savior.

Therefore, since we are surrounded by
such a great cloud of witnesses,

let us throw off everything that hinders
and the sin that so easily entangles.

And let us run with perseverance the
race marked out for us…

(12:1)

So many have gone before me, so many examples,
so many mentors from Your Word
that I have not met yet.
People of faith, not perfect, but trusting in You,
in the face of mounting pressure,
uncertainty, and suffering.

People, just like me - human, limited,
whose self-strength was nothing.

People who believed, trusted, endured, persevered,
and ran the race marked out for them,

fixing their eyes on You, their
Lord, Creator, and Savior.

Lord Jesus, enable me to throw off
hindrances to following You.

Distractions, media noise, unhelpful
habits, and behaviors.

The sin that entangles me and trips
me up - ungodly thoughts,

worldly desires, hurtful actions,
secret lusts and hatreds.

Empower me to cast all this off
and lean hard into You,

the One who has forgiven all my
past, present, and future sin.

You have set me free to run the race
You have marked out for me.

Fill me with Your strength and perseverance.

Fixing our eyes on Jesus, the pioneer
and perfecter of faith.
For the joy set before him he endured the cross,
scorning its shame,
and sat down at the right hand of the throne of God.
(12:2)

My eyes are on You, Jesus.

You will finish the work You have begun in me.

You went to the cross for me.

You shouldered my sin's penalty and died in my place.

You leaned into the cross knowing
all it would accomplish.

My Savior, Your love for me, for us, is unfathomable.

You burst forth and conquered death, for You are life.

And You sat down, mission accomplished.

It was finished.

Rivet my gaze on You, Jesus, as
I walk through this day.

Help me to lean into my cross today,

and once again die to the desire to
have life the way I want it to be,

that You might be all and everything to me.

Consider him who endured such opposition from sinners,
so that you will not grow weary and lose heart.
(12:3)

Strengthen me in my weariness and
remind me of the certainties ahead.

I want to know You, O Christ. I want You.

I am Yours. I present myself to You.

May Your will, Your desire, be accomplished
in and through me today.

In Jesus' name...

DAY 13

I'm Wearing Down
Psalm 3:5-6

Father in heaven, Lord of life,
You sustain me.
You hold me together.
You are my strength, my loving God.

I wake exhausted, O Lord.
My nights are full of fear and anxiety.
Many times I wake in a panic.
Restful sleep is hard to come by.
I feel I'm wearing down, Lord.
At night, my fear and worries descend upon me
like a heavy blanket, increasing in weight
as the night goes on, and on, and on.

I lie down and sleep;
I wake again,
because the LORD sustains me.
(3:5)

You sustain me, O Lord.
You hold me together.
You surround me.
I am in You, Jesus.
When I lie down, You are with me, in me,
and I am in You.
Give me sleep, O my Savior.
Grant rest to my aching heart,
my hurting soul,
and my anxious body.

I lie down and sleep;
I wake again, because the LORD sustains me.
I will not fear though tens of thousands
assail me on every side.
(3:5-6)

You sustain me, O Lord, You alone.
You hold me together.
Though I feel small, outnumbered, overmatched,
You are my hope and my life, Almighty One.
I give to you fears, perceived threats,
worries, concerns, burdens, and all my what-if's.
No matter what comes at me
You are still sovereign, and I am still Yours.
Nothing and no one can snatch me away
from You and Your perfect love.

I lie down and sleep;
I wake again, because the LORD sustains me.
I will not fear though tens of thousands
assail me on every side.
(3:5-6)

In Jesus' name...

DAY 14

Broken
Matthew 5:7-9

I am realizing that this world is not working for me.
It is a broken place, Lord,
and I am a broken person.
The world seems to celebrate its brokenness
by breaking itself more with each passing day.
I would prefer to heal,
and I believe that only happens through You.

"Blessed are the merciful,
for they shall receive mercy."
(5:7)

I confess I am quick to judge, evaluate, and reject.
Lord, thank You for your mercy -
Your massive, incredible, generous mercy.
Merciful Jesus who lives in me -
live through me.

"Blessed are the pure in heart,
for they shall see God."
(5:8)

You have given me a new heart, Jesus.
You have taken away my sin,
cleansed me and purified me.
One day, because of Your mercy and grace,
I will see You.

"Blessed are the peacemakers,
for they shall be called sons of God."
(5:9)

Jesus, You have given me peace with You
and peace with myself.
Let me experience this peace more and more.
Let me offer this peace, You, to those around me,
in thought, prayer, word, and action.

This world does not follow You,
though You invite all to come to You.
Though suffering, You invite me to walk with You
and live above the fray as part of Your kingdom.

Yours is an upside-down kingdom.
A kingdom of mercy, purity, and peace.
A kingdom of humility and righteousness.
The world is a noisy tyrant.
You are my suffering Savior,

Kings of kings, Lord of lords,
the Creator who holds me together
and guides my steps.
Praise be to You, O Lord.

"Blessed are the merciful,
for they shall receive mercy.
Blessed are the pure in heart,
for they shall see God.
Blessed are the peacemakers,
for they shall be called sons of God."
(5:7-9)

In Jesus' name...

DAY 15

The Noise is Deafening
Colossians 4:2

Heavenly Father, Perfect Father, Abba,
there is no one like You.
I raise my heart and soul to You today.
I praise and worship You.

Here I am, Lord, my Creator.
I give You myself. I give You this day.
Guard my heart. Guide my steps.
Remind me continually that You are with me.

Devote yourselves to prayer,
being watchful and thankful.

Lord, the noise around me is deafening.
The clamoring of my own mind can be overwhelming.
Frustration, grief, guilt, shame, and
anger gnaw at me from within.
I call out to You, my God, for help, relief, and healing.
Move me to pray - to yield myself to You.

You are compassionate, gracious, and loving.

Produce in me a life of continual
companionship and conversation with You.

I devote myself to prayer, in Jesus' name.

Devote yourselves to prayer,
being watchful and thankful.

I look for You, Jesus, for You are coming again.

I confess I often forget this.

This sure and certain hope

gets buried beneath the weight
of worries and concerns.

Cause me to eagerly wait for You, looking for You,

aware that I might see You at any moment.

In that instant, I will be transformed to be like You.

What a day that will be, my soon and coming Savior.

Maranatha! Come Lord Jesus.

Devote yourselves to prayer,
being watchful and thankful.

I think of all I've lost, and I am
stunned again by sadness.

Yet I'm amazed that I am still here, surviving.

It is clear that You have a plan for me.

Thank you, Lord. Thank you.

Cultivate great gratitude in me.

Grant me a thankful heart.

Remind me of all You have done.

Empower me to meditate on Your goodness to me.

Enable me to give thanks and to keep giving thanks.

Devote yourselves to prayer,
being watchful and thankful.

Amen. Do this in me, Lord Jesus.

Live in and through me today for Your glory.

In Jesus' name...

DAY 16

Wailing from Within
Psalm 38:8-11, 13-15

O Lord, I am weary and distraught.
I can barely lift my head.
My temples pound, my body aches.
I am filled with grief.
My soul shakes.
I wail from within.

I am feeble and utterly crushed;
I groan in anguish of heart.
All my longings lie open before you, Lord;
my sighing is not hidden from you.
My heart pounds, my strength fails me;
even the light has gone from my eyes.
(38:8-10)

I wander from place to place
in this wilderness of grief.
I am surrounded by people, yet alone.

No one seems to see me.
Perhaps I am a phantom,
merely going through the motions.

My friends and companions avoid
me because of my wounds;
my neighbors stay far away.
I am like the deaf, who cannot hear,
like the mute, who cannot speak;
I have become like one who does not hear,
whose mouth can offer no reply.
(38:11, 13-14)

At times, it seems like there is no remedy,
like there are no answers for my suffering.
How deeply the heart can hurt!
The caverns within feel bottomless,
but I know this is not so.
I know this pain is temporary and fleeting,
yet it grinds on, day after day.

Bring light to my eyes, O God.
Lift my head and relieve my distress.
Empower me with Your endurance, O Christ.
You alone are my strength. All my hope is in You.
I long for You, O Lord.

> *LORD, I wait for you;*
> *you will answer, LORD my God.*
> *(38:15)*

In Jesus' name...

DAY 17

Searching for Relief
Matthew 20:29-34

Lord, here I am, again today.
I look to You, my Maker, my Shepherd.
I bow to You, Lord of the universe -
All-wise, All-knowing, All-
powerful, Ever-present One.

Perfect Father, I feel invisible.
I have blended into the crowd,
this sea of souls frantically running here and there,
searching for relief, for meaning, for healing, for love.

As they were leaving Jericho, a large crowd followed Him.
And two blind men sitting by the road,
hearing that Jesus was passing by,
cried out, "Lord, have mercy on us, Son of David!"
The crowd sternly told them to be quiet,
but they cried out all the more,
"Lord, Son of David, have mercy on us!"
(20:29-31)

Two blind men on the outskirts of society,
viewed as unclean, beyond repair, of little to no value.
They cried out to You, Jesus, for mercy.
They knew who You were, and they called for You.
They did not care what others thought or said.
They were relentless in their search for You.
They kept calling out, persistent and passionate.
Their hope was in You.

And Jesus stopped and called them, and said,
"What do you want Me to do for you?"
They said to Him,
"Lord, we want our eyes to be opened."
(20:32-33)

Lord Jesus, sometimes I feel a bit blind.
Perhaps I am even more nearsighted than I realize.
I can be so focused on self that I cannot see You.
I can be so overwhelmed with grief and emotion,
that I do not even look for You.
Lord Jesus, have mercy on me, yet again.
Open my eyes that I might know You better,
perceive You more clearly,
and walk with You more closely.

Moved with compassion, Jesus touched their eyes;
and immediately they regained their
sight and followed Him.
(20:34)

You are full of compassion and mercy,
my Jesus, my Savior, Giver of Sight.
Heal and open the eyes of my heart.
Illuminate my blind spots and remove them.
Renew my mind and transform
me from the inside out.
Fix my eyes on You, and empower me to follow You
and to know You better with each passing day.
Cause me to trust You more, step by step.

I give You my heart, my mind, my soul, my body.
Fill me with Yourself.
Work in and through me.
Heal, renew, and cause me to rest in You.

"Lord, we want our eyes to be opened."
(20:33)

In Jesus' name...

DAY 18

Sucked into the Chaos
Colossians 3:1-4

Lord, here I am again today.
I present myself, my body and all that I am, to You.
I am Yours. You are mine.
I am in Christ, secure amid the turmoil.

I confess I am often sucked into the chaos around me,
and into the pain and grief inside me.
I get stuck in a whirlpool of thoughts and emotions,
going round and round but heading nowhere.
Have mercy on me, Jesus.
Thank you that You live in me.

Since, then, you have been raised with Christ,
set your hearts on things above, where Christ is,
seated at the right hand of God.
Set your minds on things above,
not on earthly things.
(3:1-2)

I have been raised with you, Christ Jesus.
I am alive forever with your eternal life.
Now I am always with You,
seated with You in the heavenly places,
far above all this theatrical upheaval down here.
I set my heart on You, Jesus, and on things above.
I surrender my desire to have today the way I want it
and to have life go the way I would like.

Empower me to set my mind on You, Jesus,
and on the things of You.
Focus my thoughts on the eternal
rather than the temporary.
Guard me from being hijacked
by the noise around me.
Home, finances, relationships, illnesses, work issues,
media, worries, fears, uncertainties, past wounds -
do not let me set my mind on these earthly things.
Raise my thoughts to You, O Savior.

*For you died, and your life is now
hidden with Christ in God.*
*When Christ, who is your life, appears,
then you also will appear with him in glory.*
(3:3-4)

I died with You, Jesus. I was raised with You.
Who I really am is hidden in You.
One day, perhaps very soon, You will appear.
What a glorious instant in time that will be!
You will transform me, in the blink of an eye.
You will take me up, and I will
appear with You in glory.
Yes, Lord Jesus, I yearn for that moment.
I eagerly await Your appearing.

Until then, fix my thoughts on You.
Set my heart on the things above.
Guide me again today through this grief,
this on-going, persistent suffering.

I give myself to You.
I love You. I worship You, my King,
My Creator, Savior, and Lord.

Since, then, you have been raised with Christ,
set your hearts on things above, where Christ is,
seated at the right hand of God.
(3:1)

In Jesus' name…

DAY 19

Plagued with Worry
Psalm 46:1-3, 6-7, 10

God is our refuge and strength,
an ever-present help in trouble.
(46:1)

I remind myself, LORD, that You are with me.
Fix my eyes on You.
Set my mind on You,
as I face this day with its trouble.

My mind is plagued with worry.
My heart has become a home to fear.
I seem to be afraid of everything.
I wonder where the next crisis will come from,
and when the next disaster will strike.

You are my refuge.
You are my strength.
You are my help.
You are ever-present, always with me.

Therefore we will not fear, though the earth give way
and the mountains fall into the heart of the sea,
though its waters roar and foam
and the mountains quake with their surging.
(46:2-3)

My life as I knew it is gone.
The world has changed and is changing.
I do not feel safe.
Security feels like a thing of the past.
Division, conflict, hatred, and
malice roam unhindered.
Everything feels uncertain,
as if humanity is tottering on the edge of a cliff.

Nations are in uproar, kingdoms fall;
he lifts his voice, the earth melts.
The Lord Almighty is with us;
the God of Jacob is our fortress.
(46:6-7)

You are my refuge, my strength, my help.
You are ever-present, always with me.

He says, "Be still, and know that I am God;
I will be exalted among the nations,
I will be exalted in the earth."
(46:10)

You are the LORD Almighty.
You will be exalted.
Quiet my heart. Still my soul.
Continually remind me that You are God.

God is our refuge and strength,
an ever-present help in trouble.
(46:1)

In Jesus' name...

DAY 20

Weak and Listless
Matthew 7:7-11

Lord, I am so needy.
Emotions overwhelm me.
Thoughts bounce about in my mind.
Fears assail me.
I feel weak and listless.

"Ask, and it will be given to you; seek, and you will find;
knock, and it will be opened to you.
For everyone who asks receives, and he who seeks finds,
and to him who knocks it will be opened."
(7:7-8)

Give me the strength, Lord,
to keep on asking,
to keep on seeking,
and to keep on knocking.

In my anxiety and fatigue,
help me to embrace Your promise.
I will receive what I need.
I will find what I am really seeking.

"Or what man is there among you who,
when his son asks for a loaf,

will give him a stone? Or if he asks for a fish,
he will not give him a snake, will he?

If you then, being evil, know how to
give good gifts to your children,

how much more will your Father who is in heaven

give what is good to those who ask Him!"

(7:9-11)

Forgive me, Jesus, for my lack of trust.
Wounds and grief have caused me
to doubt Your goodness.
I give these doubts and fears to You.
Help me to trust more and doubt less.

I choose to align my mind with Your Word
and what You have said about Yourself.
You are good, and Your love endures forever.
You are good, no matter what happens.
You are good, for You cannot be anything but good.
I choose to trust that You are good.

Now, good and gracious Lord,
give me eyes to see Your goodness
in the smallest things around me.
Let me notice Your continual blessings
which I usually take for granted.

"Ask, and it will be given to you; seek, and you will find;
knock, and it will be opened to you.
For everyone who asks receives, and he who seeks finds,
and to him who knocks it will be opened."
(7:7-8)

Lord, I open my hands to You.
I am completely dependent on You.
Help me, sustain me, hold me together.
Strengthen me to walk with You today.

In Jesus' name...

DAY 21

Loss After Loss
1 John 5:11-13

Lord, I seek You this morning.
I know that You are here.
Jesus, You live in me by Your Holy Spirit.
I seek You.

I cannot survive without knowing You better.
I want to trust You more, follow You more closely.
The pain and grief scream at me continually,
reminding me of loss after loss, after loss.

My life feels so dark at times,
even though You are the light.
I need Your perspective, Your love,
Your patience, Your power.
I need You.

And this is the testimony:
God has given us eternal life, and this life is in his Son.
Whoever has the Son has life;

whoever does not have the Son of God does not have life.
I write these things to you who believe
in the name of the Son of God
so that you may know that you have eternal life.
(5:11-13)

You have given me Your life, eternal life.
This life is in Your Son.
Jesus, You gave Your life for me,
so that You could give Your life to me,
so that now You might live Your life in me
and through me.
This is true, sure, and certain. This is reality.
I receive this truth and say, "Yes!"
I rest in You and Your Word.

And this is the testimony:
God has given us eternal life, and this life is in his Son.
Whoever has the Son has life;
whoever does not have the Son of God does not have life.
I write these things to you who believe
in the name of the Son of God
so that you may know that you have eternal life.
(5:11-13)

Death seems to dominate this world.
Its tentacles are everywhere and in everything.

All of life is tainted, stained, and deeply flawed.
But You, You are above all this, O Perfect Savior.
I have You, and therefore, I have everything.
I have everything I need that ultimately matters.
With broken but full heart I rejoice in You,
even as tears of grief run down my face.

I will live on these bedrock certainties,
by Your power and grace.
I have You, Jesus. You have me.
I am safe, secure, and loved, forever, no matter what.

In Jesus' name...

DAY 22

I Want Peace
Psalm 62:1-2, 5-8

Truly my soul finds rest in God;
my salvation comes from him.
(62:1)

I want rest, O God, Your rest.
I want peace - peace with You,
and peace with myself.
My soul yearns for You, O Lord.

Truly my soul finds rest in God;
my salvation comes from him.
Truly he is my rock and my salvation;
he is my fortress, I will never be shaken.
(62:1-2)

You are my rock.
I have no steadiness apart from You.
You, Jesus, are my foundation, my life.
You rescued me from sin and death.

You are my salvation.

I worship and praise You.

Though my body and emotions are shaking,

You are my fortress.

In my suffering, You surround me.

By faith, I walk with You through this wilderness.

I trust You to steady me and strengthen me today.

Yes, my soul, find rest in God;

my hope comes from him.

Truly he is my rock and my salvation;

he is my fortress, I will not be shaken.

(62:5-6)

I pour out my grief to You, O God.

From the depths of my soul I cry to You.

My hope is not in myself, nor in other people.

My hope is in You and You alone, Lord.

You are my hope.

You are sufficient for today's battles,

and for all future battles.

My salvation and my honor depend on God;

he is my mighty rock, my refuge.

Trust in him at all times, you people;

pour out your hearts to him,
for God is our refuge.
(62:7-8)

In Jesus' name...

DAY 23

Terrified of Mistakes
Matthew 5:13-16

Lord, I can barely lift my eyes to You.
I am weary and heavy with burdens.
I feel small, weak, and so limited.
I feel paralyzed, unable to make decisions.
I'm terrified of making mistakes and of more loss.

I know You are with me and in me,
yet I feel listless, lost, and purposeless.
It's as if meaning drifted out the window
during this fierce battle of grief.
I feel stuck in mourning.

"You are the salt of the earth;
but if the salt has become tasteless,
how can it be made salty again?
It is no longer good for anything,
except to be thrown out and trampled underfoot by men."
(5:13)

Me? The salt of the earth?
Salt enhances, preserves, and delights.
I feel more like a drain on You, my family,
my friends, and everyone around me.

How can I do anything good
when I can't seem to do anything at all?
I go through the motions, pretending to live,
all the while merely existing.
I'm a shadow of my former self.

*"You are the light of the world. A city
set on a hill cannot be hidden;
nor does anyone light a lamp and put it under a basket,
but on the lampstand, and it gives light to
all who are in the house." (5:14-15)*

I shake my head at this, Lord.
Your perspective is so different from mine.
I am not shining well at present, Jesus.
I wonder if I'm shining at all.
So much of life feels dark and uncertain.

Yes, I am your disciple.
I follow You, the Light of the world.
May I somehow reflect Your goodness and love,
even now, in this deep pit of grief.
Shine in me, shine through me, Jesus.

"Let your light shine before men in such a way
that they may see your good works,
and glorify your Father who is in heaven."
(5:16)

You are teaching me, O Lord,
that I am not my feelings,
nor am I my situation or circumstances.
I am Yours - Your child, Your
disciple, Your apprentice.
Things are not always what they appear.

I set my eyes again on You, Savior.
Lift me up and remind me who I am.
Focus me on You and who You are.
Give me patience and endurance for this day,
this hour, this moment.

"You are the salt of the earth...
You are the light of the world."

Shine in me, shine through me, Jesus.

In Jesus' name...

DAY 24

Decision-Making
James 4:13-16

God Almighty, Perfect Father, Lord of the universe,
You created everything, and You created me.
You wanted me. You planned me. You gave me life.
You led me to trust in Jesus.
Now I possess Your eternal life.

I look ahead, and things appear daunting.
I wonder about my ability to handle it.
Indeed, I know I can't handle it.
My self-strength is nothing.
I try to make plans, and then shake my head.
I don't know what to do. Decisions have become hard.
At times, I'm immobilized, terrified
of making the wrong choice.
I give these feelings, this decision-paralysis to You.

Now listen, you who say,
"Today or tomorrow we will go to this or that city,
spend a year there, carry on business and make money."

Why, you do not even know what will happen tomorrow.
What is your life?
You are a mist that appears for a little
while and then vanishes. (4:13-14)

Lord, these are hard words, but true.
And why do I think these are hard words?
Because they challenge my sense of control.
The old me wants to sit on the throne of my own life,
and rule over my own tiny kingdom.
It is true that I do not know what
will happen tomorrow,
or today, for that matter.
This life is indeed mist-like, fleeting, and fragile.

I give myself again to You, Lord Jesus.
You are life, and You are my life.
You gave yourself up for me,
to secure my eternity, that I might be with You forever,
and that I might walk with You today, now.
Empower me to trust and follow You.
Thank you for reminding me how fleeting this life is,
and how permanent Your life is.

Instead, you ought to say,
"If it is the Lord's will, we will live and do this or that."
As it is, you boast in your arrogant schemes.
All such boasting is evil.
(4:15-16)

I confess my arrogance, O Lord.
I boldly proclaim I am going to do this or that,
when in reality I control nothing.
Such presumption puts You on the periphery,
when Your place is at the center of all things.
Indeed, if it is Your will, I will
live - and do this or that.

I entrust to You today my mind, my heart, my body,
my life, my attitudes, my motives, my deepest desires.
I am Yours, Jesus.
Fill me with Yourself.
Live in and through me and accomplish Your will.

Instead, you ought to say,
"If it is the Lord's will, we will live and do this or that."
(4:15)

In Jesus' name...

DAY 25

Inwardly Terrorized
Isaiah 41:10

Jesus, come quickly to help me.
I am distraught, riddled with fear.
I feel inwardly torn and terrorized.
My heart braces for the next painful disaster.

So do not fear, for I am with you;
do not be dismayed, for I am your God.

Lord, I can barely think.
Words often fail me.
My heart and soul cry out to You.
I yearn for relief, and if possible, deliverance.

So do not fear, for I am with you;
do not be dismayed, for I am your God.

I hear You, O Lord.
Enable me to trust You.
I feel overwhelmed, overpowered,
out-of-control, and too scared to even hope.

So do not fear, for I am with you;
do not be dismayed, for I am your God.
I will strengthen you and help you;
I will uphold you with my righteous right hand.

I lean hard into You, Jesus.
O my Strength, strengthen me.
I feel so broken, even beyond repair.
Have mercy, Lord, for I cannot lift my head.

So do not fear, for I am with you;
do not be dismayed, for I am your God.
I will strengthen you and help you;
I will uphold you with my righteous right hand.

I give this fear to You, my Creator.
I give this terror to You, my Savior.
I give this pain, this grief to You, my Helper.
I give myself to You, my Lord and my God.

I give this day, this hour to You, my loving Father.
I give each moment to You, my merciful King.
I give all, everything to You, my Redeemer.
I choose to trust You.

So do not fear, for I am with you;
do not be dismayed, for I am your God.

I will strengthen you and help you;
I will uphold you with my righteous right hand.

In Jesus' name...

DAY 26

What's Next?
Matthew 6:25-34

"Therefore I tell you, do not worry about your life,
what you will eat or drink; or about
your body, what you will wear.
Is not life more than food, and the
body more than clothes?
Look at the birds of the air;
they do not sow or reap or store away in barns,
and yet your heavenly Father feeds them.
Are you not much more valuable than they?
Can any one of you by worrying
add a single hour to your life?"
(6:25-27)

I worry about many things, Lord.
I confess I worry about almost everything.
How did I get here? Who am I now?
What's the purpose of all this?
What do I do? What's next?

"And why do you worry about clothes?
See how the flowers of the field grow.
They do not labor or spin.
Yet I tell you that not even Solomon in all his
splendor was dressed like one of these.
If that is how God clothes the grass of the field,
which is here today and tomorrow is thrown into the fire,
will he not much more clothe you—you of little faith?"
(6:28-30)

Thank you, Lord, for providing for me.
Thank you for food, clothing, air to breathe,
a heart that beats, a functioning mind,
water, clothing, shelter...
Thank you.

"So do not worry, saying,
'What shall we eat?' or 'What shall we
drink?' or 'What shall we wear?'
For the pagans run after all these things,
and your heavenly Father knows that you need them.
But seek first his kingdom and his righteousness,
and all these things will be given to you as well."
(6:31-33)

I know that worry is fruitless.
It accomplishes nothing and only adds to my trouble.

I want to trust You instead.
Trust more, worry less.

I have a worry list stuck in my mind.
I give that list to You.
I confess my worries and fears.
Be first, O Lord, in my heart.

Be first, Jesus.
Your kingdom. Your righteousness.
Your will. Your plan.
Fill me with Yourself.
Cause worry to fade into the background.

"Therefore do not worry about tomorrow,
for tomorrow will worry about itself.
Each day has enough trouble of its own."
(6:34)

Today, Jesus. Just today.
Help me walk with You today.

In Jesus' name...

DAY 27

On the Brink of Despair?
1 John 2:15-17, 28

Lord, sometimes I feel this world has nothing for me.
It promises much but delivers almost nothing.
What it does give is false and fleeting.
It does not satisfy.
It cannot give the contentment I long for.

My feelings and thoughts scare me a bit.
I wonder if I am going crazy.
Am I depressed and heading in the wrong direction?
Am I losing hope and on the brink of despair?

Do not love the world or anything in the world.
If anyone loves the world, love for
the Father is not in them.
For everything in the world—
the lust of the flesh, the lust of the
eyes, and the pride of life—
comes not from the Father but from the world.

(2:15-16)

Thank you, Father. I am relieved.

No wonder I am not content here.

No wonder I feel as I do and have these thoughts.

I have loved this world and made it my god.

The result was always more than disappointing.

Then I turned around and blamed You
for not coming through for me,

even as I worshipped the world and myself.

Empower me to release this world
for what it is - empty.

I agree with You, Perfect Father, my Creator.

Jesus, You modeled this for me.

You chose the love of the Father, and Your love for me,

over the voices of this world.

The world and its desires pass away,
but whoever does the will of God lives forever.
(2:17)

I think of investing for the future.

Every financial advisor talks about
the importance of this.

Yet so often I have not invested in my real future,
my eternal future with You.

I give my desires, all of them, to You, Lord.

Give me what You desire for me.

You alone know me and what is best for me.

Help me to trust You, to let go, and to rest in You.

And now, dear children, continue in him,
so that when he appears we may be confident
and unashamed before him at his coming.
(2:28)

Lord Jesus, live through me.

Produce Your fruit in me and fulfill Your plan for me.

You are near. You could come any day.

Prepare me and help me look forward
with eager anticipation.

Make me ready and keep me ready.

Come, Lord Jesus.

In Jesus' name...

DAY 28

A Jumble of Emotion
Psalm 103:1-5

Praise the LORD, my soul;
all my inmost being, praise his holy name.
(103:1)

In my suffering, I praise You.
In my pain and grief, I raise my eyes to You.
I am a jumble of emotion, O God.
You know this and welcome me.
I am Yours. You are mine.
I praise You, Lord.

Praise the LORD, my soul,
and forget not all his benefits—
(103:1)

How can I list Your benefits?
You thought of me and wanted me.
You planned me and created me.
You gave me life and provided for me.

You cause my heart to beat
and give me the air I breathe.
Everything I have and everything good
I have experienced has come from You.
I praise You, O Lord.

Who forgives all your sins
and heals all your diseases,
who redeems your life from the pit
and crowns you with love and compassion...
(103:3-4)

You have taken away my sins.
You have cleansed me with the
precious blood of Christ.
Your sacrificial love endured my penalty on the cross.
Then You conquered death for me.
You are my physician,
and all the healing I have known is a gift from You.
You have rescued and delivered me more times
than I can count and more than I even know.

Forgive me when I question Your goodness.
I confess this to You.
My pain overwhelms and even blinds me at times.
All this You know, and here You are, with me.
Enable me, Lord, to appreciate and experience
Your infinite compassion and love for me.

Who satisfies your desires with good things
so that your youth is renewed like the eagle's.
(103:5)

Lord, You are always blessing me.
In my grief, Your love never ceases nor diminishes,
even though I can't seem to taste it as I would like.
And so I trust, for trust is my only way through this.

I praise the LORD, O my soul,
and all that is within me.
I praise Your holy name.

In Jesus' name...

DAY 29

Desperate for Love
Proverbs 29:25

The fear of man will prove to be a snare,
but whoever trusts in the LORD is kept safe.

I confess that for almost my entire life,
I have feared other people.
Desperate for love, I have performed,
people-pleased, conformed, and complied.

I have defined myself by what others said and did,
by how they treated me, and by
what they wanted from me.
I let the world mold and shape me
into habits and patterns that kept You at a distance.

I didn't know it, but I was in bondage.
I was searching, performing, placating,
appeasing, demanding,
trying to find myself somehow, somewhere.
All I needed to do was to come home to You.

The fear of man will prove to be a snare,
but whoever trusts in the LORD is kept safe.

I confess I have had many idols.
I have worshipped things, hopes, dreams, and people.
I have worshipped myself.
I put on my little crown and ruled my paltry kingdom.

Thank you, Jesus, that You have brought me home -
home to You and to Your love and Your life.
Thank you for Your forgiveness.
Thank you for Your complete acceptance.

Living for an audience of people was exhausting,
frustrating, angering, meaningless, and futile.
I now seek to live for an audience of One.
I seek to live for You and You alone.

The fear of man will prove to be a snare,
but whoever trusts in the LORD is kept safe.

I abandon the fear of people.
Empower me to trust You, more and more.
Jesus, You are my safety and security.
You are my provision, my salvation, my life.

Remove my idols, Lord, one by one.
I surrender them all to You.
I relinquish my self-made crowns
and my miniscule kingdom.
I follow You.

In Jesus' name...

DAY 30

All is in Upheaval
John 16:33

Lord, all is in upheaval -
my life, my relationships, the world.
All is craziness and confusion.
I do not know how to think.
I do not know what to do.

My inner turmoil rages.
My mind spins relentlessly.
My heart quakes within me.
My body trembles.
Uncertainty increases by the day.

Jesus, I remember that You said:

*"I have told you these things,
so that in me you may have peace.
In this world you will have trouble."*

Honestly, Lord, I don't want any more trouble.
I've had enough pain, grief, and suffering.

I know this world is broken, fallen, and reeling.
I'm tired of it all. Exhausted.
I have no strength left.

Then again, this is not about me and my strength.
It's about You and Your plan - Your strength.
You speak to me through Your Word.
You speak through what You've spoken.
You offer me peace through believing
what You have said.

*"I have told you these things, so that
in me you may have peace.
In this world you will have trouble."*

You have spoken to me through Your Word,
that I might have peace -
not peace in my abilities, circumstances, or finances,
but peace in You.

I have peace in You. You are my peace.
At times, I have trouble experiencing this peace,
but that doesn't change the fact
that I have peace in You.
Cause me to shift my thinking from fear to trust.
I choose to rest in You,
and trust that I will experience Your peace.

*"I have told you these things, so that
in me you may have peace.
In this world you will have trouble.
But take heart! I have overcome the world."*

I will take heart today, whether or
not my emotions follow.
I will take heart, because I know You.
I am in You, Jesus, and You are in me.
You have overcome the world, and I am in You.
That means I also have overcome the world.

I cling to You and Your Word.
I choose to abide in You and what You have said.
I receive Your promises and all that You have for me.
I want to know You, Christ, my Savior,
my Lord, Creator of the universe, my Friend.

*"I have told you these things, so that
in me you may have peace.
In this world you will have trouble.
But take heart! I have overcome the world."*

In Jesus' name...

DAY 31

Have Mercy
1 Thessalonians 4:16-18

Have mercy on me again today, Lord.
I will not make it without You.
Indeed, I am dependent upon You for my every breath
and for every beat of my grieving, hurting heart.

O Lord Jesus, I wait for You.
You are here. You are in me, and I in You.
Yet I wait for You, to see You,
to be transformed to be like You.

*For the Lord himself will come down from
heaven, with a loud command,
with the voice of the archangel and
with the trumpet call of God,
and the dead in Christ will rise first.*
(4:16)

This day is coming,
just as certain as the next moment is coming.
You have promised, and You will do it.
All that's left is the timing. And so I wait.

Encourage me in the waiting, Lord Jesus.
On that day, all who have died and believed in You
will rise, in new bodies, to live forever with You.
Some of these people I know, and
I smile when I think of
the joy, delight, and wonder of that moment.

*For the Lord himself will come down from
heaven, with a loud command,*
*with the voice of the archangel and
with the trumpet call of God,*
and the dead in Christ will rise first.
After that, we who are still alive and are left
*will be caught up together with them in the
clouds to meet the Lord in the air.*
And so we will be with the Lord forever.
(4:16-17)

After the dead are raised, those who
are alive and have trusted in You
will be transformed in an instant to be like You,
with new bodies, glorified, never again
to know pain, decline, or illness.
Gone will be infirmities, griefs,
conflicts, and estrangements.
No more struggles with our own
sin or the sins of others.

We will become, finally, all that
we were designed to be.
It is beyond my comprehension.
It will be far better than I can
possibly dream or imagine.

Therefore encourage one another with these words.
(4:18)

Thank you, Lord, for encouraging my heart.
Throughout this day, and every day,
remind me of your coming –
Your soon and imminent appearing.
It could be today. Yes, any day.

I present to You my body, soul, and spirit - all of me.
I release to You once again my
sorrows, pain, and grief.
Put all these in perspective for
me, Lord of all, as I wait.
Keep me looking up, watching for You.

In Jesus' name...

THE THIRD MONTH

DAY 1

The End of Myself
Psalm 116:1-7

I love the LORD, for he heard my voice;
He heard my cry for mercy.
Because he turned his ear to me,
I will call on him as long as I live.
(116:1-2)

I call upon You today, Lord.
You see me. You hear me.
You know me.
Here is my heart.
Here are my thoughts and feelings.
Here I am.
I entrust myself to You.

The cords of death entangled me,
the anguish of the grave came over me;
I was overcome by distress and sorrow.
Then I called on the name of the LORD:
"Lord, save me!"
(116:3-4)

This has played out time and again in my life.
I have come to the end of myself many times.
I thought my life was ebbing away.
Several times I thought my time had come.
Other times I wished that it were so.

Through every distress and sorrow,
You have been the one constant.
You were always there -
embracing, loving, and strengthening me,
even when I could not feel Your presence.

You have saved me, Jesus.
You have saved me from sin and death.
You have rescued me from an eternity apart from You.
Deliver me today from selfish thoughts
and wayward, godless ways.
I want to live in conscious and continual
companionship with You.

The LORD is gracious and righteous;
our God is full of compassion.
The LORD protects the unwary;
when I was brought low, he saved me.
Return to your rest, my soul,
for the Lord has been good to you.
(116:5-7)

You have indeed been good to me.

All true good I have experienced has come from You.

You saved me. You have given me rest.

You will give me rest.

In Jesus' name...

DAY 2

Plenty to be Afraid Of
Genesis 15:1

After this, the word of the LORD
came to Abram in a vision:
"Do not be afraid, Abram.
I am your shield, your very great reward."

"Do not be afraid."
You say this often, Lord.
We humans clearly have an issue with fear,
and with good reason.
There is plenty to be afraid of
in this fallen, bent world full of selfishness,
deception, cruelty, and injustice.
You tell me again today, *"Do not be afraid."*

I bring to You the fear lurking in my heart.
I fear being abused and taken advantage of.
I fear being rejected, cast off, and abandoned.
I fear more emotional and physical pain.
I fear something terrible happening.

I fear what I dread coming to pass.
I fear that You will not come through for me.
I fear being completely lost.

After this, the word of the Lord
came to Abram in a vision:
"Do not be afraid, Abram.
I am your shield, your very great reward."

I fear being vulnerable and weak.
I fear being a victim, again.
I fear what has happened will happen again.
I fear what might be or could be.
I fear not being protected the way I would like.
I fear having to go through terrible suffering.
I fear death and the dying process.
Help me, O Lord, my Shield.

After this, the word of the Lord
came to Abram in a vision:
"Do not be afraid, Abram.
I am your shield, your very great reward."

All my fears are surrendered,
as best as I know how.
I cast myself upon You, Sovereign God.
Lord Almighty, I trust that You are always at work,

even now, blessing, loving, and maturing me.

All praise be to You,

Lord Jesus, Almighty God,

Savior of the world.

In Jesus' name...

DAY 3

Growing Numb
John 15:5

Lord, I fear my heart is shutting down.
Things are too emotional, and I'm overwhelmed.
I'm growing numb,
and that scares me.

I feel distant from You.
I know You are here, but I feel so far away.
I don't know who I am anymore.
I fear I'm losing myself in all this.

"I am the vine; you are the branches."

Jesus, I am connected to You.
You are the source of my life.
You are the source of everything good.
I have Your life, eternal life, inside me.
I know these things to be true,
though at present I do not feel them as I would like.
Truth is not based on my feelings, thank goodness.
Your Word is truth. You are truth.

"I am the vine; you are the branches.
If you remain in me and I in you,
you will bear much fruit..."

Lord, not only do I not feel fruitful,
I feel purposeless.
I feel adrift without a sense of meaning.
I feel lost and terribly lonely,
even though You live in me, and I live in You.
Again, feelings. More feelings.
I fear I have made feelings my
god, an idol of some sort.
Lord, I entrust my feelings to You.

"I am the vine; you are the branches.
If you remain in me and I in you,
you will bear much fruit;
apart from me you can do nothing."

I receive Your Word today, Jesus.
You are my home. I abide in You.
I am a home of Yours. You abide in me.
Your life pulses inside me.
Produce Your fruit in my life, Lord,
even amid all this pain.
Use every bit of this grief and suffering
for Your purposes.

"I am the vine; you are the branches.
If you remain in me and I in you,
you will bear much fruit;
apart from me you can do nothing."

I am joined to You, Jesus.
Thank you, thank you, thank you.
Cause me to rest in You, my Savior.
You are sufficient for all and everything
that I am facing and will face.
Again today, I die to the way I
would like for things to be.
Again today, I take up my cross and follow You.
Apart from You, I can do nothing.

In Jesus' name…

DAY 4

Stark Reality, Certain Hope
1 John 5:19-21

I praise You, Lord of heaven and earth,
though my heart trembles and my soul writhes,
though the world quakes and fears surround me,
though all seems dark, even lost.

*We know that we are children of God,
and that the whole world is
under the control of the evil one.*
(5:19)

What clear truths. What stark realities.
I rejoice that I am Your child, a follower of Jesus.
I shake at the next reality and
wonder if I heard it correctly.
The whole world is under the control of the evil one?

I must let this sink in. I read it again.

The whole world is under the control of the evil one.
(5:19)

I look at the world. Yes, I can see this.

Sin, pain, suffering, and death.

Abuse, cruelty, slavery, and trafficking.

Wars, divisions, violence, hatred, and murder.

Conflicts, estrangements, betrayals,
and rampant deception.

Self-centeredness, narcissism,
oppression, and genocide.

We know also that the Son of God
has come and has given us understanding,
so that we may know him who is true.
And we are in him who is true by
being in his Son Jesus Christ.
He is the true God and eternal life.
(5:20)

We know also - thank goodness for that *also* -
You have come, Jesus. You are the remedy.
You have given us true understanding –
understanding that can come only from You.
What's the key to surviving, even thriving,
in this dark world?
Knowing You, Jesus.
You are true. You are the truth.
Though the evil one rages, I am in You.
You are the Victor, and You live in me.

The evil one is active, but he is beaten.
You defeated him once and for all on the cross.
He brings only death,
but You have conquered death forever.
Fix my eyes, heart, and mind on
You, Conquering Savior.

Dear children, keep yourselves from idols.
(5:21)

Focus my heart, Lord Jesus.
Protect me from diminishing who You are,
and from chasing after things of this world.
You alone are worthy. I worship You.

I am Yours, Lord Jesus.
Take all of me today.
Again, I give You my heart, mind, soul, body.
Live through me for Your glory.

In Jesus' name...

DAY 5

Trying to Run
Psalm 131:1-3

Lord, here I am.
I keep trying to figure this out.
I keep trying and trying to get it right.
I keep doing the same things.
I keep expecting different results.

I take things on myself.
I try to do it all.
I somehow think it's about me.
I keep trying to run from this pain,
to fight this suffering.
I exhaust myself in the process.
I often find myself frozen in grief.

You are God. I am not.
How many times do I have to learn this?
Perhaps it's a layer-of-the-onion type thing?
I confess my selfish, self-focused efforts.
Help me, O Lord.

My heart is not proud, Lord,
my eyes are not haughty;
I do not concern myself with great matters
or things too wonderful for me.
(131:1)

King David wrote these words,
which makes them even more stunning.
He had such ability and power,
and yet he saw the fallacy of self-trust and self-effort.
Help me follow his lead, O God.

I relinquish all to You.
I entrust to You difficulties,
decisions, worries, and fears.
I release quandaries, conflicts,
disappointments, and offenses.
I give You all wounds, pains, griefs, and suffering.
I entrust to You possessions, health,
finances, and reputation.
I give You my family, relatives,
friends, and all relationships.
I entrust to You my life and all that it contains.

But I have calmed and quieted myself,
I am like a weaned child with its mother;
like a weaned child I am content.
(131:2)

I set aside the noise of this world -
the constant barrage of info and messages.
Empower me to do this, Jesus,
and to pursue Your way.
Live through me in love, peace,
patience, and kindness.

Jesus, You laid down your life out of love,
and yet the world continued on its destructive path.
I choose You and Your way today.
You live in me, Jesus. Live through me.
Accomplish Your purpose and Your will in me today.

You alone provide contentment.
Your way alone is the path to contentment.
Yet it's not about contentment but about You.
May I seek You more than Your limitless benefits.

I plan for peace today.
I seek You and Your peace amid the challenges.
This day will have trouble in it.
So be it. This is still Your day.

My heart is not proud, Lord,
my eyes are not haughty;
I do not concern myself with great matters

> *or things too wonderful for me.*
> *But I have calmed and quieted myself,*
> *I am like a weaned child with its mother;*
> *like a weaned child I am content.*
> *Israel, put your hope in the LORD*
> *both now and forevermore.*
> *(131:1-3)*

In Jesus' name...

DAY 6

No End to the Pain
Hebrews 13:6

O Lord, my Rock, my Fortress,
You are my Shield and my Stronghold.
You are my Refuge.
I rest in You, my Creator and my Savior.
I lift my eyes to You,
Lord and Creator of all.
I am Yours, for You made me.
I belong to You.

My heart is sad today, O Lord.
I grieve over all that has happened
and over all that is happening.
There seems to be no end to the pain,
the fear, the suffering, and the grief.
This storm is relentless and severe.
I am worn out from the constant assault
upon my heart, mind, soul, and body.

So we say with confidence,
"The Lord is my helper;

I will not be afraid.
What can mere mortals do to me?"

I can do nothing apart from You, Lord.
I confess the complete inadequacy of my self-strength.
I control nothing.
You created and redeemed me.
Lord Jesus, I have received many wounds
from others, even those I counted on.
Even friends and some family treat me like a shadow,
as if I am invisible and unworthy of their attention.

You are my Rock and my Salvation.
You alone. You and no other.
The help of man, if not sent by You, is worthless.
People can be unfeeling, callous, even mean.
The cruelty of some words and actions is stunning.
Uncaring, they shatter already broken hearts,
and don't lift a finger to support or comfort.
Hearts have grown cold.

So we say with confidence,
"The Lord is my helper;
I will not be afraid.
What can mere mortals do to me?"

Remind me, O God, that what others do and say
is about them and not about me.

They cannot hear my grief.

They do not want to see my pain.

I fear that one day I will be left completely alone,

and yet I know this is impossible.

You, Jesus, are in me, and I am in You.

Let me experience continual,

close fellowship with You today.

So we say with confidence,
"The Lord is my helper;
I will not be afraid.
What can mere mortals do to me?"

In Jesus' name...

DAY 7

Never Alone
Psalm 139:1-10

You have searched me, Lord,
and you know me.
You know when I sit and when I rise;
you perceive my thoughts from afar.
You discern my going out and my lying down;
you are familiar with all my ways.
(139:1-3)

You are always with me, Lord.
I am always with You.
You know everything in all creation.
Your knowledge is complete and total.
Nothing is hidden from You.
Help me, Lord, to bring everything into the light.
May Your love overpower my fear and hesitancy.

Before a word is on my tongue
you, Lord, know it completely.
You hem me in behind and before,

and you lay your hand upon me.
Such knowledge is too wonderful for me,
too lofty for me to attain.
(139:4-6)

You know my heart, my mind, my soul, my body.
You know all that goes on within me.
You know my joys, rejections, wounds, griefs,
delights, sins, motives, and desires.
You surround me.
In You I live and move.
Let Your complete knowledge comfort me.
Reassure me and strengthen me.

Where can I go from your Spirit?
Where can I flee from your presence?
If I go up to the heavens, you are there;
if I make my bed in the depths, you are there.
If I rise on the wings of the dawn,
if I settle on the far side of the sea,
even there your hand will guide me,
your right hand will hold me fast.
(139:7-10)

Thank you, Lord, that though
I can attempt to run from You,
I cannot succeed.

Your love holds me fast.
Your commitment to me is total.
I am not faithful, but You are.
I trust that You are healing me.
Heal my soul, heart, mind, and body.

I need Your rest, Your peace.
You are my rest.
You are my peace.
Fill me and comfort me, O God.

In Jesus' name...

DAY 8

I Toss and Turn
Psalm 139:11-14

There are days I would rather not get out of bed.
Lord, You know I do not sleep.
I toss and turn.
I doze and wake.
My mind never stops.
My heart never settles.

In the darkness, I cry out to You.
At times, my heart goes silent,
too afraid to show itself.
Sometimes I feel I'm withering away on the inside.
Life can be so lonely.
Even sunny days can be dark.

If I say, "Surely the darkness will hide me
and the light become night around me,"
even the darkness will not be dark to you;
the night will shine like the day,
for darkness is as light to you.

(139:11-12)

You are here, Lord.

You are in this darkness with me.

You never leave me.

You created me. You saved me.

You redeemed me from slavery to
sin, self, and the world.

You hold me together, moment by moment.

Nothing can separate me from
You or Your love for me.

Nothing. Ever.

For you created my inmost being;

you knit me together in my mother's womb.

I praise you because I am fearfully
and wonderfully made;

your works are wonderful, I know that full well.

(139:13-14)

I do not see myself as you see me.

Only You see me correctly.

Only You know who I truly am.

Thank you that I am not my wounds.

I am not what has happened to me.

I am not my grief.

I am not my losses.

I am Your creation. I am Your child.

I have value beyond imagining
because of You.

Today, in the dark, I remember You.
I am quiet in Your presence, listening.
You are here, with me.

In Jesus' name...

DAY 9

What's the Purpose?
Psalm 139:15-18, 23-24

Lord, there are some days when I am morose.
The heaviness of life, grief, and a
broken heart press in upon me.
I can barely breathe.
My mind begins to run through my losses,
and I soon find myself wondering
why I am here and what the purpose of all this is.

Before I disappear into this personal pit,
remind me of Your Son.
Remind me of the cross.
Remind me of the empty tomb.
Pierce this mental fog with Your light.
Remind me who I am.

My frame was not hidden from You
when I was made in the secret place,
when I was woven together in the depths of the earth.
Your eyes saw my unformed body;

all the days ordained for me were written in Your book
before one of them came to be.
(139:15-16)

I am not an accident.
I am not a random product of human reproduction.
You declare that I am more than this.
I believe You, for I feel it deep inside.
I was made for You, for eternity.

You made me. Personally.
You wanted me.
You created me for Yourself.
You made me for Your purposes.
You know all of my life, all my days here -
from beginning to end.

How precious to me are your thoughts, God!
How vast is the sum of them!
Were I to count them,
they would outnumber the grains of sand—
when I awake, I am still with you.
(139:17-18)

You are amazing.
I cannot fathom You.
You are better than my mind can conceive.
You do not waste pain and suffering.

You know all of it, and I believe You feel it with me. Jesus, You know all about suffering and grief.

Search me, God, and know my heart;
test me and know my anxious thoughts.
See if there is any offensive way in me,
and lead me in the way everlasting.
(139:23-24)

In Jesus' name...

DAY 10

It is Finished
John 5:24-25

"Very truly I tell you,
whoever hears my word and believes him who sent me
has eternal life and will not be judged
but has crossed over from death to life."
(5:24)

Lord Jesus, I have heard Your Word.
I believe the One who sent You, the Father.
I trust in You and all that You have done for me.
You remind me today that eternal life
is not something I will have,
but something I already possess, here and now.
You have promised that I will not be judged.
You have been judged in my place.
You took my penalty and died my death.

"Very truly I tell you,
whoever hears my word and believes him who sent me
has eternal life and will not be judged

but has crossed over from death to life."
(5:24)

I have eternal life, Jesus, because I have You.
Eternal life is Your life.
I have crossed over from death to life.
Crossed over - past tense.
It is done. It is finished.
You have done it all,
and I am the recipient of all You have done.
Amid this suffering, I possess Your life.

I have experienced so many deaths.
I seem to experience more every day -
the loss of this, the loss of that.
The loss of dreams, expectations, hopes, abilities,
strength, beauty, perceived identity,
friendships, relationships, family, people,
and a sense of safety and security.
With deaths and losses everywhere,
I cling to You and Your life.

Very truly I tell you,
a time is coming and has now come
when the dead will hear the voice of the Son of God
and those who hear will live.
(5:25)

I close my eyes and smile.
Yes, Lord, yes.
I was dead. I heard Your voice.
I trusted You. Now I live.
And the day will come, Your Day,
when You appear and all those who trusted You
throughout history will hear Your voice, rise, and live.

Someday, this will all be over.
Suffering will be done and gone.
Until that day, I will persevere
through Your strength and power,
day by day, moment by moment.
I will remember that I have eternal life now,
and that I am living Your life today.
Live through me, Lord Jesus.

"Very truly I tell you,
whoever hears my word and believes him who sent me
has eternal life and will not be judged
but has crossed over from death to life."
(5:24)

In Jesus' name...

DAY 11

Thirsty Soul, Hungry Heart
John 6:68, Hebrews 12:4,
2 Timothy 3:16-17

Holy Father in heaven, Creator of all that exists,
You are holy, holy, holy.
There is no one like You, none besides You.
From everlasting to everlasting, You are God.

My soul is thirsty, Lord.
My heart hungers for so much,
but I know it really hungers for You.
Open my heart to You today.

Simon Peter answered Him,
"Lord to whom shall we go?
You have the words of eternal life."
(John 6:68)

Jesus, You alone have the words of eternal life.
You are the Word, and all things were created
by You and for You and through You.

You have spoken, and You are speaking
through what You've spoken.

For the word of God is alive and active.
Sharper than any double-edged sword,
it penetrates even to dividing soul and
spirit, joints and marrow;
it judges the thoughts and attitudes of the heart.
(Hebrews 4:12)

You are life. Your words are life.
Your Word is alive.
Pour Your Word into my heart, heal my broken places.
Comfort me, sustain me, strengthen me,
according to Your perfect will and plan for me.

All Scripture is God-breathed and is useful
for teaching, rebuking, correcting and
training in righteousness,
so that the servant of God may be thoroughly equipped
for every good work.
(2 Timothy 3:16-17)

Your Word - Your very breath, O Sovereign God,
I hold in my hands.
How miraculous. How marvelous.
Let Your words sink in, deep into my innermost being,

and bring Your spiritual health, wisdom, and healing.

I confess I listen to many words every day -
the words of others, messages here,
there and everywhere.
Yet I am slow to come to You and listen.
I neglect the fact that Your Word is my daily bread.

Here I am, Lord.
Here is my heart, my mind, my body, my pain,
my grief, my anger, my frustrations, my fears.
Take it all, Lord Jesus.

In Jesus' name...

DAY 12

True Peace
John 14:27

Lord, I can barely look up today.
My heart is heavy and hurting.
The pain and grief seem to increase by the moment.
Have mercy on me, O Lord.

Peace I leave with you; my peace I give you.

Peace sounds unbelievably good.
It's hard to imagine what peace would feel like
amid this continual pressure of suffering.
I wonder what will come at me next.
I fear the slightest breeze will tip me into oblivion.
I have no strength to stand, Lord.
I am barely existing, so far from living.
I'm afraid to hope. I cannot bear
any more disappointment.

Peace I leave with you; my peace I give you.

Jesus, I know You.

You say I have Your peace already. I have it now.

If that's true, then I will have your peace
the next moment and tomorrow also.

Your peace must be different than I imagine.

It must be peace-in-the-midst-of, peace-in-spite-of,

peace-even-though this and peace-even-with that.

You say that if I have You, I have Your peace.

How much I experience it is another thing altogether.

Peace I leave with you; my peace I give you.
I do not give to you as the world gives.

I'm reminding myself again – I have You, Jesus.

Since I have You, I have Your peace,

You have given Your peace to me.

You Yourself are my peace,

my security, my acceptance, my meaning, my life.

Lift my heart, my Savior, and open my soul

to experience more of You, more of Your peace.

May I taste peace-even-though
this, peace-in-spite-of that,

and peace-because-of-You,

Savior, Lord, God Almighty.

Peace I leave with you; my peace I give you.
I do not give to you as the world gives.
Do not let your hearts be troubled and do not be afraid.

Enable me, Jesus, to trust You,

even when I feel anything but peaceful.

Help me believe that I already have Your peace,

and that I will feel and experience
it at the proper time.

I just want to experience it now, Lord, always now.

I am so fearful, distraught, and worried.

You know all this, and so I cast myself upon You.

I cling to You.

You are my peace.

Peace I leave with you; my peace I give you.

I do not give to you as the world gives.

Do not let your hearts be troubled and do not be afraid.

In Jesus' name...

DAY 13

Feeling the Pain of the Past
Psalm 32:7-9

Lord of heaven, Creator of all things,
my Maker, Sustainer, Redeemer, and Savior –
I worship You. I praise You. I adore You.
Thank You for Your mercy and goodness.

Pour more mercy out on me today, O King.
Remind me of all You've done –
Your goodness and Your love.
My wounds have bubbled up to the surface today.
I am feeling the pain of the past in the present.

You are a hiding place for me;
You preserve me from trouble;
You surround me with shouts of deliverance.
(32:7)

Hide me in You, Almighty One.
Shelter me from this terrible storm.
Trouble is everywhere, and my strength is waning fast.

Protect me. Provide for me. Preserve me.

My life depends on You, as it always has.

Surround me, encompass me, hold me fast,

in this ever-flowing current of suffering.

Raise me up and deliver me, O God.

I will instruct you and teach you
in the way you should go;
I will counsel you with my eye upon you.
(32:8)

I hear Your voice and these promises, Lord.

You will instruct me. You will teach me.

You will guide me in the way I should go.

You will counsel me.

I release again my desire to control, to deliver myself,

to figure it all out and to fix everything.

I confess my utter inability to do
anything apart from You.

I yield. Help me to yield more.

Your eye is upon me.

You know me. You know everything.

Your plan for me is perfect.

You are perfect. Increase my faith and trust.

Be not like a horse or a mule, without understanding,
which must be curbed with bit and bridle,
or it will not stay near you.
(32:9)

I smile and sigh at this verse, Lord.
This is me. I stubbornly resist You in many ways.
Many times, I am proud and defiant.
I wander from You and resist You more than I realize.
You remind me that I am Your child.
You remind me to come, to share,
to pour out my heart, and to trust You.
All my deepest needs are already met in You, O Christ.

You are a hiding place for me;
You preserve me from trouble;
You surround me with shouts of deliverance.
(32:7)

I release all to You, my Faithful Savior.

In Jesus' name...

DAY 14

From the Depths of the Pit
Lamentations 3:55-57

O Lord my God, Creator of all that is,
King of kings, and Lord of lords,
You are holy, holy, holy.
I worship and adore You, my Father.

Though I have You, my Lord, I seek You.
I rise today and keep on seeking You.
Do not let me be deterred by the noise blaring at me,
and the avalanche of information coming at me.
I give my unruly emotions to You.
I give You my mind, my racing thoughts.
I give You my doubts, fears, and worries.
Have mercy and empower me again today, my Savior.

I called on your name, LORD,
from the depths of the pit.
You heard my plea:
"Do not close your ears to my cry for relief."
You came near when I called you,
and you said, "Do not fear."

You see me.
You hear my voice, my heart, my soul.
You know me completely.
I present myself to You, all of me.
Amid fear, enable me to choose faith.
Amid pain, empower me to choose peace.
Amid uncertainty, strengthen me to cling to You.
Amid the noise, tune my heart to Your voice.

I release to You these burdens.
I entrust to You this sadness, anger, fear, guilt,
all the anxieties and unknowns.
Teach me what is real, sure, and certain.
My heart and mind yearn for peace.
You, Jesus, are my peace.
I long for certainty, stability, and safety.
You, Jesus, are all this and much more.

I called on your name, LORD,
from the depths of the pit.
You heard my plea:
"Do not close your ears to my cry for relief."
You came near when I called you,
and you said, "Do not fear."

I rest in You, Jesus, Savior.
Fill me with Yourself, with Your Spirit.

Live through me and accomplish Your purposes.
I trust in You.

In Jesus' name...

DAY 15

Invisible
John 13:34

O Lord God, there is no one like You.
You spoke and things came to be.
Awesome Creator, All-powerful One,
merciful, gracious, compassionate, loving,
You bless us. You bless me,
again and again, moment by moment.
All life comes from You.
I am Yours. I bow before You, Lord Almighty.

O my Strength, my Maker, my heart aches
and writhes with pain and disappointment
from losses, hurts, and rejections.
Some brothers and sisters in Christ do not see me.
They cannot seem to hear my heart.
They do not want to be in the
presence of my suffering.
Some feign concern and spout platitudes -
meaningless and empty words for this wounded heart.

"A new command I give you: Love one another.
As I have loved you, so you must love one another."

That is my problem, Lord. I do not feel loved.
I feel invisible, cast off, and desperately lonely,
like a resident of some island in
the middle of nowhere,
where no one else dares to come.
I feel abandoned. I even feel betrayed.
Is it me, O Lord? Is there something wrong with me?
I just want to be accepted, loved, heard, and seen.
Is that too much to ask?

"A new command I give you: Love one another.
As I have loved you, so you must love one another."

You have loved me, Jesus, and You love me still.
You gave yourself for me.
How many times have I turned from You,
ignored You, and distanced myself from You?
How often have I desperately tried to
make life work on my own?
Yet You loved and pursued me,
relentless in Your care and compassion,
constantly inviting me to rest in You
and experience Your love.
Perhaps I am looking to others for what

You alone can provide.
Only You can provide full and complete acceptance,
perfect love, no matter what.
Have I made idols out of the people around me?
Have I been looking to them to meet my needs
instead of to You?

*"A new command I give you: Love one another.
As I have loved you, so you must love one another."*

By Your grace, empower me to let You be You,
and to let people be people.
I forgive those who have hurt me.
I release them and give up being offended.
I will look to You to meet my needs,
for You are the only One who can.
Instead of seeking to be loved and understood,
I will seek to love and understand.

Lord Jesus, You remind me that apart from You
I can do nothing.
I cannot do this, or anything, in my own strength.
Live through me, Lord,
and love those around me as only You can do.

*"A new command I give you: Love one another.
As I have loved you, so you must love one another."*

I look to You alone, O Jesus, my Savior.
You are my Creator, Almighty God,
Prince of Peace, my coming King.
I worship and adore You.

In Jesus' name...

DAY 16

Everything Seems Different
Ecclesiastes 2:22-25

I love You, Lord Jesus.
You are with me.
You never leave me.
You go before this day, and all days.

I am anxious today, Lord.
It seems I'm anxious a lot, maybe all the time,
about so many things - perhaps about everything.
Everything seems different.
My world has been altered.
People seem different. I seem different.
Life seems different.
Different, different, different.
I feel confused, shaky, unstable.

What do people get for all the toil and anxious striving
with which they labor under the sun?
(2:22)

I have wondered about this.
So many times, my efforts were disappointing.
Failures were devastating.
Great achievements did not satisfy.
I kept at it - working, pushing, striving,
hoping to somehow arrive somewhere.
But where? My own Garden of Eden?
Some place free of uglies, messes, and pain?

What do people get for all the toil and anxious striving
with which they labor under the sun?
All their days their work is grief and pain;
even at night their minds do not rest.
This too is meaningless.
(2:22-23)

I walked around smiling, but inside
anger, disappointment, pain, and grief were churning.
I kept slamming the lid shut, hiding the truth,
keeping up the ruse, and lying to myself and others.
My mind spun in perpetual circles,
trying to crack the code of happiness.
I thought if I could just get it right, all would be well.
It was all up to me, of course.

Fruitless. Meaningless. Exhausting. Empty.

Gary Roe

*A person can do nothing better than to eat and drink
and find satisfaction in their own toil.
This too, I see, is from the hand of God,
for without Him, who can eat or find enjoyment?
(2:24-25)*

Lord, all truly good things come from You.
You bless, love, provide, and protect,
even when I am spinning.
Even when I am striving and
pushing my own agendas.
Lord, I have placed You on the periphery,
while I tried to play captain of my own life.
But my life is not my own.
I belong to You.
You have given me life and everything else.

I am not God. You are.
You wanted me and created me.
Only You know who I truly am.
You have a plan for me, a good plan.
I abandon my own happiness plans
and give myself anew to You and to Your plan.
I look to You for the love, peace,
hope, and contentment
that only You can provide.

In Jesus' name…

DAY 17

Decisions Seem Impossible
John 10:7-10

Lord, I do not know what to do.
I do not know how to feel.
Simple decisions seem impossible.
Conflicting messages are everywhere.

Therefore, Jesus said again,
"Very truly I tell you, I am the gate for the sheep."
(10:7)

Jesus, tune my ear to Your voice.
Focus my heart on You.
You know all things, and You know me.
You are wise. Your love is perfect and infinite.
You are the gate, my gate.
You are the way in. You are the way.
My eyes are on You.

"All who have come before me are thieves and robbers,
but the sheep have not listened to them."
(10:8)

This world is full of lies, and I have
believed many of them.

Much of my life has been stolen by
falsehoods and untruths.

Not everyone has my best interests in mind.

Teach me to discern between truth
and error, Lord Jesus.

Lies cause suffering and destruction.

You are the truth.

Fix my eyes on You.

"I am the gate; whoever enters through me will be saved.
They will come in and go out, and find pasture."
(10:9)

Jesus, You are my Shepherd.

I have entered life, eternal life, through You.

I am part of your flock.

My sins are forgiven.

You live in me, and I live in You.

You have provided for me.

Provide for me.

My eyes are on You.

"The thief comes only to steal and kill and destroy;
I have come that they may have life,
and have it to the full."
(10:10)

I hide myself in You, Lord.
You are my rock and my fortress.
You are my salvation and my life.
You have brought me into Your life, Jesus.
I now possess Your life, eternal life.
You conquered sin on the cross.
You rose and conquered death.
You are victorious and I am in You.

Though grief, pain, and suffering persist,
they will not last forever.
Praise be to You.
Fix my eyes on You, Jesus.

In Jesus' name...

DAY 18

No Condemnation
Romans 8:1

O Lord, You are always with me.
I cannot hide or run from You.
You know me, You see me.
You hear me, You hold me.

Life feels overwhelming, my Father.
I am terrified by what is and what might be.
I am in try-to-control-everything mode.
I feel faithless, rebellious, and unworthy
of even a glance from You.

Therefore, there is now no condemnation
for those who are in Christ Jesus...

My guilt is heavy and stifling.
I am plagued by all I have done and not done.
I cringe at all I've said and not said.
I look back and see failure upon failure, sin after sin.
I am nauseated by my lack of faith.

I doubt Your goodness, Your love,
and even Your care for me.
In my shame, I try to hide myself from You.

*Therefore, there is now no condemnation
for those who are in Christ Jesus...*

I confess all this to You, my loving Savior, Jesus.
You hung on the cross for me.
You died in my place and bore all my penalty.
You took all my sin - past, present, and future.
I receive Your complete forgiveness
and cleansing again today.
Though I'm burdened, You remind me that I am free.
I am loved. I am accepted.
I am cherished by You, Jesus, my Lord.

*Therefore, there is now no condemnation
for those who are in Christ Jesus...*

Amid the pain, I remember You.
Amid the grief, I know that I am Yours.
I am in You, Christ Jesus, and You are in me.
You will hold me up and comfort me.
You will support and encourage me.
You are my strength, my hope, my life.

There is no condemnation for me, because of You.

I love You, Lord Jesus.
I praise You this day.
I follow You today,
step by step, moment by moment.

In Jesus' name...

DAY 19

Waiting
Psalm 130:1-6

Out of the depths I cry to you, LORD;
LORD, hear my voice.
Let your ears be attentive
to my cry for mercy.
(130:1-2)

Here I am, Lord, again today.
My heart, my soul, my body are all before You.
You know every emotion, every thought,
every inclination and twitch of my heart.
You know every loss, every wound,
every bit of suffering, every grief.
I pour it all out before You.

If you, LORD, kept a record of sins,
LORD, who could stand?
But with you there is forgiveness,
so that we can, with reverence, serve you.
(130:3-4)

You and You alone, Lord, enable me to stand.
Jesus, You took my sins on Yourself.
You died my death and paid my penalty.
You conquered death and gave me Your life.
My future is safe and secure in You.

Cleanse me afresh now, Lord.
Bring to mind things I have not yet confessed
so that I might release them to You.
I receive once again Your forgiveness.
I want to live in the freedom that You won for me.
I want to walk in the freedom of Your Spirit,
loving and serving You.

How can I serve You with this pain?
How can these wounds honor You?
You turn ashes to beauty.
You turn suffering into eternal fruit.
Take all my grief, Lord, and use it for Your purposes.
Turn the pain into something beautiful.
I don't understand this, but I see the cross.
I trust You.

Help me to trust You more.

I wait for the LORD, my whole being waits,
and in his word I put my hope.
I wait for the LORD

more than watchmen wait for the morning,
more than watchmen wait for the morning.
(130:5-6)

In Jesus' name…

DAY 20

Well Past My Limits
Romans 8:15

Loving Father, King of the universe,
There is no one like You.
You are Lord over all.
I worship You, my Rock.

I feel I am on shifting sand, Lord.
I can't seem to get my footing in life.
Things are not what they were.
I am not who I was.
I'm frightened about what's coming,
though I don't know what that is.
I fear more pain and suffering are ahead.
I'm afraid I'm already well past my limits.

The Spirit you received does not make you slaves,
so that you live in fear again;
rather, the Spirit you received brought about
your adoption to sonship.
And by Him we cry, "Abba, Father."

You remind me that You, Almighty God, dwell in me.
You have placed me in Your Son, Jesus,
and now Your Spirit, You Yourself, dwells in me.
Your Spirit whispers, "I have You. You are mine."

You rescued me from my pit of sin and shame.
You delivered me from darkness into light.
You transferred me from the kingdom of
death into Your Kingdom of Life.
I hear Your Spirit again whisper, "You are mine."

You know my fears. Take them from me.
You know my anxious thoughts. Renew my mind.
You know my fatigue. Give me grace and more grace.
You have adopted me. I am Yours forever.

The Spirit you received does not make you slaves,
so that you live in fear again;
rather, the Spirit you received brought about
your adoption to sonship.
And by Him we cry, "Abba, Father."

All earthly fathers are imperfect,
and some are much better fathers than others.
You, however, are the original, the perfect Father.

Perfect in love. Perfect in compassion.
Perfect in patience.
Perfect in wisdom. Perfect in everything.
Let me not judge You by earthly fathers,
for You are in a class all by Yourself.
Infinite. Incomprehensible. Righteous. Loving.

I confess, Abba, that I have judged
You by circumstances,
by what has happened to me and around me.
In this broken world permeated by sin and suffering,
we manage to make a ruin of our own lives.
Yet we rage against You.
We blame You, while enjoying blessing after blessing.
Everything truly good is ultimately from You.
I confess I have made You a target
for my angst and anger.

The Spirit you received does not make you slaves,
so that you live in fear again;
rather, the Spirit you received brought about
your adoption to sonship.
And by Him we cry, "Abba, Father."

I release this frustration, anger, and angst to You.
I embrace You today as my Abba - my Father.
You love me with Your perfect love.

You paid my adoption price with Your blood, Jesus.

I am now Your child and part of Your family forever.

This is my identity - child of God.

I am not this suffering.

I am not this grief.

I am not my current circumstances,
whatever they might be.

Your Spirit, Abba, lives in me.

I am Yours, Abba.

I trust in You.

In Jesus' name...

DAY 21

My Soul Shakes
Isaiah 44:8

Lord, I turn my eyes to You.
My heart feels crushed. I yearn for You.
My mind is muddled. I long for Your peace.
I know You see me, Lord.
See me.

I look ahead and all is foggy.
Challenges and demands fill my ears,
while the world bombards me with fear.
I trust in You, and yet my soul shakes.

"Do not tremble, do not be afraid.
Did I not proclaim this and foretell it long ago?
You are my witnesses.
Is there any God besides me?
No, there is no other Rock; I know not one."

I give my trembling mind and heart to You.
I give these fears, anxieties, and uncertainties to You.

It is beyond me to handle and manage all this.

I give all to You.

You know all things, Lord God, Almighty One.

You know all that was, is, and what is to come.

All knowledge and all wisdom are Yours.

Nothing surprises You.

You know all that is ahead.

In Your wisdom and power, You
have revealed the future.

You have told us what is yet to come.

You want to prepare us and strengthen us.

Prepare me, O Lord.

Strengthen me. Deepen my faith.

Enable me to cling to You and rest in You,

confident in Your plans for me.

"Do not tremble, do not be afraid.

Did I not proclaim this and foretell it long ago?

You are my witnesses.

Is there any God besides me?

No, there is no other Rock; I know not one."

Lord, expose my idols,

the things I trust in and worship

to help me feel better and prop me up.

I forsake my own self-strength and wisdom.

My abilities are woefully inadequate.
You, however, are sufficient for all things -
every day, every hour, every minute,
every challenge, every threat, every fear.

You are my Rock. There is none like You.
You are my Fortress. There is none besides You.
You alone are the Lord Almighty. You alone are God.
All others are but pretenders, mere smoke in the wind.

You are eternal, unchanging, all-powerful.
You are loving, compassionate, forgiving, and good.
You are true, faithful, generous, and merciful.
You are holy, righteous, just, and sovereign.

"Do not tremble, do not be afraid.
Did I not proclaim this and foretell it long ago?
You are my witnesses.
Is there any God besides me?
No, there is no other Rock; I know not one."

My eyes are on You, Lord God Almighty.
I am Yours. You are mine.
I praise and worship You,
Lord of life, King of creation.

In Jesus' name…

DAY 22

Not Who I Was
Romans 8:38-39

O Lord, I trust that You are with me.
Jesus, better than just being with me,
You live in me, and I live in You.
I am one spirit with You.
You are my life, my hope,
my security, my stability,
my anchor in this tossing sea
of fear, anxiety, uncertainty, guilt, and grief.

I feel attacked and trapped, Lord.
My relationships are not what they were.
People are not what they were.
I am not who I was.
Everything seems to have changed,
except for You, my Anchor in this storm.
I know what yesterday was,
but I do not know what today will be.
Fear lurks, ready to pounce.

For I am convinced that neither death nor life,
neither angels nor demons,
neither the present nor the future, nor any powers,
neither height nor depth, nor
anything else in all creation,
will be able to separate us from the love of God
that is in Christ Jesus our Lord.

My failures stare at me in the mirror.
Hurt, wounds, and rejections pound my restless soul.
I try to force myself through the days,
the hours, the minutes,
to establish some kind of order in this chaos.
Help me, Jesus, my Savior, my Lord.
You are my peace. I choose to abide in You.
You know all about storms,
and You have authority over them all.

For I am convinced that neither death nor life,
neither angels nor demons,
neither the present nor the future, nor any powers,
neither height nor depth, nor
anything else in all creation,
will be able to separate us from the love of God
that is in Christ Jesus our Lord.

Nothing and no one can separate me
from You and Your perfect love for me.
I am fully and completely Yours.

You did this - You did it all.
I contributed nothing.
You contributed everything.
I receive this truth again today,
and embrace You with all I am.

For I am convinced that neither death nor life,
neither angels nor demons,
neither the present nor the future, nor any powers,
neither height nor depth, nor
anything else in all creation,
will be able to separate us from the love of God
that is in Christ Jesus our Lord.

Jesus, You are my life.
I present myself to You again this day.
Work Your will in and through me.
Be glorified, O Risen Savior.

In Jesus' name...

DAY 23

All Power is Yours
Daniel 2:20-22

I lift my eyes and heart to You, O God.
Raise my thoughts to You.
I give You my heart, my mind, my soul, my strength.
I present myself to You. You are God, my God.

"Blessed be the name of God forever and ever,
to whom belong wisdom and might."
(2:20)

All wisdom belongs to You.
All power is Yours. You are the Almighty One.
All wisdom I have comes from You.
All my strength is ultimately Yours.

"He changes times and seasons;
He removes kings and sets up kings;
He gives wisdom to the wise
and knowledge to those who have understanding."
(2:21)

You are the Creator and Sustainer of all nature.
Times and seasons march along
according to Your command.
Rulers govern by Your permission.
Though things appear to be falling apart,
You are still sovereign and working out Your plan.
Wisdom and understanding are gifts from You.
Everything that is good comes from You.
I praise You, King of the universe.

He reveals deep and hidden things;
He knows what is in the darkness,
and the light dwells with him."
(2:22)

Nothing is hidden from You.
Nothing can separate me from You -
no pain, no loss, no suffering, no one, nothing.
You are the light. You shine.
You reveal what I need to know
to follow You, to trust You.

I open my clenched fists today.
I raise these open, empty hands to You.

"Blessed be the name of God forever and ever,
to whom belong wisdom and might.

He changes times and seasons;
He removes kings and sets up kings;
He gives wisdom to the wise
and knowledge to those who have understanding;
He reveals deep and hidden things;
He knows what is in the darkness,
and the light dwells with him."
(2:20-22)

Here I am, Lord.
I surrender to You.

In Jesus' name...

DAY 24

In Suffering, Rest
John 19:28-30

Perfect Father, my Creator,
I look to You again today.
I have no strength left in myself.
You are my strength,
and Your strength is infinite and measureless.
In this struggle, in this storm of storms, I cling to You.
In this suffering, I rest in You,
as my heart aches.

Later, knowing that everything had now been finished,
and so that Scripture would be fulfilled,
Jesus said, "I am thirsty."
A jar of wine vinegar was there,
so they soaked a sponge in it,
put the sponge on a stalk of the hyssop plant,
and lifted it to Jesus' lips.
(19:28-29)

O Lord Jesus, I cannot fathom or even imagine
the suffering You endured.

I treat the cross so lightly at times.

You, Creator of the universe, died there for me.

The exposure. The mocking. The abuse.

The torture and pain.

The unfathomable agony of becoming my sin,

of becoming everyone's sin,

And of receiving in Yourself our penalty.

Suffering Savior, I love You.

There is no one like You.

You know, Lord. You know.

You have me and will not let go.

You will never leave me or forsake me.

No one and nothing can separate me from You.

I live in You, my Savior, for You are life.

You are my life.

When he had received the drink,

Jesus said, "It is finished."

With that, he bowed his head

and gave up his spirit.

(19:30)

Thank you, Jesus, thank you.

It is finished, it is done.

You did it. You did it all.

I contributed nothing,

for I had nothing whatsoever to contribute.

I receive all You have done.

I receive You, O Conqueror of sin and death.

I follow You, Suffering Savior.

You go before me today.

You go with me.

You are in me. I live in You.

Fill me with Your Spirit,

that all of life might be companionship with You.

You walk with me. You enable me to walk with You.

You are the Light, my Light,

on this dark, difficult road.

"It is finished."

In Jesus' name...

DAY 25

Life is So Brief
Psalm 103:13-19

Lord, Perfect Father, Creator,
There is no one like You.
You are my life and my salvation.
Deliver me from all my fears.

As a father has compassion on his children,
so the LORD has compassion on those who fear him;
for he knows how we are formed,
he remembers that we are dust.
(103:13-14)

You know me, Abba, Father.
You know my frailties, my weaknesses,
my vulnerabilities.
You surround me, my Shield.
I am your child, O Compassionate One.

The life of mortals is like grass,
they flourish like a flower of the field;

the wind blows over it and it is gone,
and its place remembers it no more.
(103:15-16)

Life is so brief and my time so limited.
I was only born yesterday,
and my years have flashed by like some shooting star.
I grieve for making so much of my life about me.

But from everlasting to everlasting
the LORD's love is with those who fear him,
and his righteousness with their children's children—
with those who keep his covenant
and remember to obey his precepts.
(103:17-18)

I bow before You, my Creator, my Savior.
Your love is strong, steadfast, infinite, and eternal -
just like You, Almighty, Sovereign Lord.
I surrender myself to You again today.
I entrust to You my feelings, my
thoughts, my decisions,
my motives, my words, my actions.
You are with me, every moment, every step.
Your love and righteousness surround me.

The LORD has established his throne in heaven,
and his kingdom rules over all.
(103:19)

Though I cannot see it, Perfect Father,
I trust that You are working in all things
for my good and for Your glory.
You are incomprehensible, holy, righteous,
pure, just, good, and eternal.
All-powerful. All-knowing. All-wise. Ever-present.
You are upon Your throne.
I praise You.

In Jesus' name...

DAY 26

Not a Friendly Place
Matthew 5:10-12

Lord, the world has never been a friendly place
for those who follow You,
for those who take Your Word seriously,
and seek to love You with their whole being.

Today I am mindful that this world rejected You,
and continues to do so.
Yet I am shocked when it rejects me,
and acts like I don't even exist.

*"Blessed are those who have been persecuted
for the sake of righteousness,
for theirs is the kingdom of heaven."*
(5:10)

Lord, the pain inside is great.
Comfort and console me, Jesus.
Remind me that when I am
misunderstood and rejected
that I am in good company.

Let me not be moved, dear Lord.
Let me be content in You
and in all that comes from following You.
Strengthen my shaky soul.

"Blessed are you when people insult
you and persecute you,
and falsely say all kinds of evil
against you because of Me."
(5:11)

The world insults, reviles, and mocks.
Fueled by fear, anger, and hatred,
it blames and accuses.
Evil spreads like a contagion.

Jesus, remind me that the world is not just responding
to me but to You in me.
Though this may add to my grief,
let me also experience the joy
that comes from walking closely with You.

"Rejoice and be glad,
for your reward in heaven is great;
for in the same way
they persecuted the prophets who were before you."
(5:12)

Yes, I am in good company.

I belong to You, Jesus.

Praise You, Creator, King, Lord, and Savior.

This too shall pass.

I will rejoice and be glad in You.

In Jesus' name...

DAY 27

Perfect Peace
Isaiah 26:3-4

Perfect Father, Lord of Creation, Ruler of all,
You are the first and the last,
the Alpha and the Omega,
the beginning and the end.
There is truly no one like You.

I praise You, though all around me churns and heaves,
and though my own soul trembles.
My feelings want to reign over me.
Unwanted thoughts clamor for attention.
I look to You, O Lord, Infinite One.
Remind me of Your truth, of what is real,
and give me perspective.
Quiet my noisy, quivering heart.

You will keep in perfect peace
him whose mind is steadfast,
because he trusts in You.
(26:3)

Perfect peace, not just the peace of relief.
Perfect peace, not merely temporary tranquility.
Perfect peace, not just a passing calm amid the storm.
Perfect peace, lasting peace, true peace.

Peace from You. Peace only You can give.
You give peace and can keep me in perfect peace.
Fix my mind on You.
Make my mind steadfast, focused on You.

You will keep in perfect peace
him whose mind is steadfast,
because he trusts in You.
(26:3)

My mind feels scattered and fragmented.
My heart wanders and chases things that don't matter.
Worry and fear cloud my vision.
My lust for control is staggering,
and I can't seem to shake it.

I give myself - all of me - to You again today.
You know my thoughts, emotions,
inclinations, and motives.
Cleanse and purify my mind and heart.
May my desire be for You - You above all else.

You will keep in perfect peace
him whose mind is steadfast,
because he trusts in You.
Trust in the LORD forever,
for the LORD, the LORD Himself,
is the Rock eternal.
(26:3-4)

Keep me in Your perfect peace, Lord.
Jesus, You are my peace.
Your Spirit dwells in me, and I live in You.
You alone are God, and there is no other.
I trust in You.
Increase my trust, day by day.
Grow Your peace in me.
My Creator and Savior, I adore You.

You will keep in perfect peace
him whose mind is steadfast,
because he trusts in You.
(26:3)

In Jesus' name...

DAY 28

Dying to Live
John 12:23-26

Perfect Father, Creator and Lord of all,
I belong to You.
You made me. You redeemed me.
I am Yours.

I quiver inside with all that is happening.
I get so lost so quickly
in worry, fear, and even terror
of what might be or could possibly be
down this dark, challenging road of
whirlwind emotion, grief, and pain.

Jesus replied, "The hour has come for
the Son of Man to be glorified.
Very truly I tell you, unless a kernel of
wheat falls to the ground and dies,
it remains only a single seed.
But if it dies, it produces many seeds."
(12:23-24)

You talk about death, Lord - Your death.

A single death that produces life.

Life not just for one or some, but for many.

Your death led to life - eternal life for me

and for all who trust in You alone for salvation.

You showed me the way by dying.

You call me to follow You - and die.

This is Your way, the way of the cross.

"Anyone who loves their life will lose it,
while anyone who hates their life in this world
will keep it for eternal life."
(12:25)

O Jesus, I struggle.

I grip everything so tightly-

what I have, what I want, and even what I've lost.

I stubbornly cling to my failing self-strength,

believing that I can somehow be self-sufficient.

I absurdly, tenaciously grasp the illusion of control.

I buy the lie that I can somehow
fashion the life I want

if I just figure things out and do it all right.

I am deceived by the myth that if I can just change
myself, circumstances, and other people,

all will somehow be well.

You call me to follow You - and die.

You invite me to join You on the way of the cross,

where You surrender all and everything.

You died, so that I might now have
eternal life and live free

by dying to my insane thirst for control.

You offer me freedom from this self-tyranny,

self-deception, self-focus, and self-worship.

Enable me to trust You and let You be my life.

"Whoever serves me must follow me;
and where I am, my servant also will be.
My Father will honor the one who serves me."
(12:26)

I serve You, Jesus. I follow You.

This means that I take up my cross daily.

I die today to my desire to control things and people.

I die today to the desire that I
must have the life I want.

I want You, Jesus. I want You.

I want You to be all and everything to me.

You are with me, in me. I am in You.

And I will be where You are, forever.

Until then, I die daily,

so that You might live in and through me

as unhindered as possible.

Loving Savior, may it be unto me just as You wish.

In Jesus' name...

DAY 29

The World is Not Getting Better
Revelation 21:1-4

O Lord, have mercy on me again today,
for I am discouraged and afraid.
The world is not getting better.
Things are falling apart. Evil is advancing.
Darkness is encroaching everywhere.
My heart is apprehensive of what will happen,
and how I will manage to cope.
I feel so weak, so limited, so small.

Then I saw a new heaven and a new earth,
for the first heaven and the first earth had
passed away, and the sea was no more.
And I saw the holy city, new Jerusalem,
coming down out of heaven from God, prepared
as a bride adorned for her husband.
And I heard a loud voice from the throne saying,
"Behold, the dwelling place of God is with man.
He will dwell with them, and they will be his people,
and God himself will be with them as their God.

He will wipe away every tear from their
eyes, and death shall be no more,
neither shall there be mourning, nor
crying, nor pain anymore,
for the former things have passed away."

I lift my eyes and heart to You.
I have a secure and certain future.
I will be directly in Your presence.
When Jesus appears, I will be transformed forever.

All this - this pain, grief, suffering, and fear -
will be gone in an instant.
I will be exactly who You created me to be.
I will be more alive than I have ever been before.
No more mourning. No more grief.
No more crying or weeping. No more pain.
The former things will pass away.
All is in Your capable, all-powerful hands.

In the meantime, I accept this struggle.
I look to You, my Creator and Savior.
I will not trust in my own strength.
I will depend on You and Your strength,
O Inexhaustible One.
You hold me. You will not let me go.
No one can snatch me away from You.

Nothing and no one can separate me
from the love of Christ.
I am perfectly loved, accepted, forgiven, free,
and secure forever.

I give myself to You, O Jesus.
I yield to You, my Perfect Father.
Fill me and live through me, Holy Spirit.
I am Yours.

And I heard a loud voice from the throne saying,
"Behold, the dwelling place of God is with man.
He will dwell with them, and they will be his people,
and God himself will be with them as their God.
He will wipe away every tear from their
eyes, and death shall be no more,
neither shall there be mourning, nor
crying, nor pain anymore,
for the former things have passed away."

In Jesus' name...

DAY 30

Staying Ready for Jesus
1 John 3:1-3

Perfect Father, Lord of my life,
I know Your love is perfect, infinite, and eternal.
Yet I am forlorn, and I wonder about so much.
My experience of Your love is so meager and small
compared to the reality of its immensity and power.
Have mercy on me, O God, and somehow enable me
to experience more of Your great love.
My heart yearns for this, Lord.

See what great love the Father has lavished on us,
that we should be called children of God!
And that is what we are!
The reason the world does not know
us is that it did not know him.

(3:1)

You remind me that, though You
planned and created me,
I have not always been Your child.

Before I came to know Your Son, Jesus,

I was lost in sin, in bondage to
self, the world, and Satan.

I rejected You as God and as the
rightful Lord of my life.

You broke through my sin, my hardness of heart,

my stubborn pride.

You lovingly conquered my resistance
with Your kindness.

Your patience with me was, and is, astounding.

I am now a child of Yours.

This is who I am.

Your love made this possible.

The world I live in rejects all this.

No wonder I struggle at times.

Dear friends, now we are children of God,
and what we will be has not yet been made known.
But we know that when Christ appears,
we shall be like him, for we shall see him as he is.
(3:2)

I am Your child forever,

but I am not yet what I will be.

When You appear, Jesus, I will be changed.

I will be changed completely, forever transformed.

I will see You and be made like You.
I will be finally and forever conformed to Your image.
I will see You, Jesus. I will see You.
What a moment that will be!
No more sin, no more pain, no more struggle.
The fight fought. The race finished. The victory won.

All who have this hope in him purify themselves,
just as he is pure.
(3:3)

Now is temporary.
My feelings and moods shift like shadows.
Why do I put so much stock in emotions
and allow them to control me?
Instead, empower me to look for You, Jesus.
Remind me to eagerly wait for Your appearing,
perhaps even today.

Cause me to live today as fully as possible,
in the power of Your Spirit.
Prepare me.
When You appear,
may You find me ready and waiting.
Keep me ready, Lord Jesus.

In Jesus' name...

DAY 31

Releasing All

1 Corinthians 6:19, Matthew 6:33, Luke 14:27, Jude 24-25

Here I am, my Perfect Father, Heavenly King,
Creator, Savior, my Lord and God.
There is no one like You.
I will have no other gods besides You.

Those who unite themselves with the Lord
are one with Him in spirit.
(1 Corinthians 6:19)

You have led me. You will lead me.
You are faithful, even if I am faithless.
O Christ Jesus, You live in me, and I live in You.
I am one spirit with You, today and every day.

But seek first the kingdom of God
and all these things will be added to You.
(Matthew 6:33)

I release all things to You.
I entrust to You my will and decisions,
my mind and my thoughts,
my emotions and feelings.
I entrust to You my body and my physical health,
my future, my hopes, my dreams,
and my expectations.
I entrust to You my family, my friendships,
my relationships, my abilities,
and everything I have and possess.

And whoever does not carry his cross
and follow me cannot be my disciple.
(Luke 14:27)

Strengthen me to carry my cross.
I die today to my desire for life to be like I want it.
I give to you all pain, grief, anguish, and suffering.
I know, believe, and trust that You will use all
for my good, for Your glory,
according to Your perfect plan.
I worship and adore You.
I give thanks to You in all circumstances,
for You are always at work beyond what I can perceive.

To him who is able to keep you from stumbling
and to present you before his glorious presence
without fault and with great joy—
to the only God our Savior be glory, majesty,

power and authority, through Jesus Christ our Lord,
before all ages, now and forevermore! Amen.
(Jude 24-25)

Protect me, O Lord, from stumbling.
I look forward to seeing You face-to-face.
I long to be fully redeemed and transformed.
I yearn to be ushered into Your holy presence forever.
All praise be to You, Father, Son, Holy Spirit,
God Almighty, Ruler of all.

In Jesus' name...

CONCLUDING
THOUGHTS

Our souls need to cry out.

The Lord is listening. His love for you is perfect. He is perfect.

Soul Cry was written to be repeated. You can simply go back and start again. If you wish, you can use this prayer devotional continually, from here on out.

In 1 Thessalonians 5:16-18, the Lord gave us some simple but profound commands through the Apostle Paul:

> *Rejoice always. Pray without ceasing. Give thanks in all things for this is God's will for you in Christ Jesus.*

Rejoice always. Pray continually. Give thanks in all things.

Though life is hard and often painful, we have much to rejoice about. Our pain and grief, however, can be so noisy and intense that we cease to look in the direction of our present and future blessings.

We must make a commitment to rejoice - and to rejoice always. For most of us, this is going to be a new habit. It's going to take time and persistence. But we can start today.

Praying without ceasing seems impossible, and yet that's the command. We are to live life in conversation with the Almighty - a constant, never-ceasing conversation. Continual communication and companionship with the Lord.

We must decide to pursue a lifestyle of prayer. We must ask

the Lord to empower us to pray continually. We must ask and keep asking.

Give thanks in all things. We can always give thanks. It's a choice - a heart choice.

Rejoicing. Praying. Giving thanks. These are three things the Lord uses to guard our hearts from being completely hijacked by personal pain, trauma, and life circumstances. No matter what is happening, we can still choose to rejoice in the Lord, to seek Him in prayer, and to give thanks.

I can't close without this pastoral admonition - please, above all else, immerse yourself in the Word of God.

His is the voice you need to hear. His Word is more powerful than you can imagine. Begin the day with His Word. End the day with His Word. Find ways to permeate your daily life with His Word.

We live in days of great deception. His Word is truth. Anchor yourself in Him and His Word, more than ever.

Cry out. God is listening.

Take heart. Jesus has overcome the world, death, and Satan.

Rest. God has you.

Rejoice. Christ Himself lives in you.

And one day, you will see Him face to face.

Maranatha. Come Lord Jesus.

GARY'S STORY

Thank you for reading *Soul Cry*. I hope you found these pages comforting, encouraging, healing, and faith-building. If you haven't already, I hope you will embrace Jesus soon. In fact, I'm praying for you right now.

Please make sure you grab your free download *What in the World is Going On (and What's Coming Next)?* We live in extraordinary times. God has revealed history in advance through the prophecies in His Word. He wants you to know what's ahead. He wants you to be prepared, so that you might trust in Him during these challenging days.

Again, here's the link to
*What in the World is Going On
(and What's Coming Next)?*
https://www.garyroe.com/what-in-the-world

A CHILDHOOD OF LOSS

My story began with an early childhood of mixed messages and sexual abuse. There were multiple perpetrators and the abuse continued for several years. All the perpetrators were family members. This skewed everything - how I viewed family, people, life, and God. Throughout my childhood I felt dirty, damaged, and different.

I lost both grandfathers so early I barely remember them. Due to dementia, one grandmother never knew who I was. My parents' marriage was strained and volatile. I never knew what to expect. Looking back, I can see that my mom had been slipping into mental illness for a long time. Though I had relatives nearby, she managed to keep us isolated. I felt sad and lonely most of the time.

My family experienced other close losses, and I can still feel the atmosphere of grief that blanketed our home. It was stifling and had a tinge of hopelessness to it.

I decided I wanted to go to church. I was about 10. I somehow always knew God existed, but I wanted to know more about Him. More than that, I wanted to know Him. I knew I needed to know Him if I was going to make it.

After reading some of the Bible, Jesus became very real to me. I could almost see Him in front of me - inviting me to come into His arms. I asked Him to forgive me, cleanse me, and save me.

In junior high school, a good friend died suddenly over the Christmas holidays. He sat right in front of me in homeroom. He was bright, fun, full of promise, and healthy. I began each school day staring at his empty desk.

My mom continued to decline mentally. My parents separated and divorced in my early teens. By default, I stayed with Mom. She slipped deeper and deeper into a world of grandiose delusions. She had a breakdown and was hospitalized.

I moved in with Dad. The next six months were great. Dad was stable. His presence provided a strong sense of safety.

Then one Sunday afternoon, Dad collapsed in front of me of

a massive heart attack. They were able to resuscitate his heart, but he never regained consciousness. I sat by his hospital bed, held his hand, and said everything I could possibly think of to say. I gazed at his face for long periods of time, as if trying to memorize it. I knew in my heart he was already gone. Once they turned off life support, he died a few hours later.

After Dad's death, Mom was even more unstable than before. She attempted to take her own life and was placed into inpatient psychiatric care.

My world, as I knew it, was over. I was 15.

A TOTAL LIFE SHIFT

In my simple teen way, I accepted reality. Life was difficult. Bad stuff had happened. Yet, all of this was more than I could handle. My anxiety and anger started to leak out. I began engaging in risky behavior. Some of my friends wondered if I had a death wish.

During all this, I knew that Jesus was there. I knew He was with me, but I honestly didn't pay much attention. I was trying to slog through everything on my own.

After living alone for a few months (I still don't know how that happened), one of my best friends and his dad showed up at my door. "We want you to come live with us." I had known them for 10 years. I had been in their home numerous times. Easy decision.

From the moment I walked into their home, I felt a profound sense of safety. Even though they already had four kids, they loved, accepted, and supported me in every way imaginable. It was so good, in fact, that I simply couldn't take it all in.

One day, I asked the dad why they would take in a kid like me. He smiled and said, "Gary, with what Jesus Christ did for us, how could we not do this for you?"

I already knew Jesus, but now I was experiencing His love for me in new and profound ways through my new family. For me, it has never been about religion or going to church. It's always been about relationship with Jesus. I had a relationship with Jesus, but now I began to learn what it meant to trust and follow Him.

I went to college and studied psychology. Not surprisingly, my adult life has been about helping hurting people heal and grow by finding and walking with Jesus. As I give, I heal a little bit more.

"A father to the fatherless, a defender of widows, is God in his holy dwelling. God sets the lonely in families..." (Psalm 68:5-6a).

I have experienced the truth of these words many times. Everywhere I went, God created a sense of family for me. I have been blessed indeed.

THE LOSSES KEPT COMING

As I got older, the losses continued to pile up, as they do with all of us. I lost more relatives, friends, and co-workers. With each loss, the pain of past losses came visiting and added to the grief of the present. As a missionary and pastor, I was frequently around emotional pain, grief, and loss.

Then my marriage of almost three decades ended in a divorce I did not want or agree with. The pain and confusion were intense. For the next several years, I questioned almost everything. The death of my marriage was devastating.

Amid all the pain, God was faithful. He saw me through. He empowered me as a single dad. At a time when I thought my ministry life was tarnished and over, He kept giving me more and more ministry. My first three books were published during this time.

When I seek God, wait, and don't try to make something happen, God surprises me. My heart warmed to an amazing lady who had lost her husband to cancer. We dated and then married. And just after my youngest daughter graduated from high school, I inherited four more kids.

Even with all the new goodness, this last decade has been wracked with loss after loss. Life never stops. The challenges and difficulties keep coming.

And now the world itself has turned upside down. Fear, anxiety, anger, and uncertainty seem to be in the atmosphere we breathe.

LIFE IN A CRAZY WORLD

Yet God has not changed. He is the steady anchor amid this relentless storm. Jesus knows all about storms. Jesus knows all about hardship, pain, rejection, false accusation, loneliness, separation, and death. He endured it all, bore my sins and yours, and died in our place. Then, He conquered death. He is victorious. He is life.

And He is coming back for those who have trusted Him.

If you do not yet know Him, please don't delay. He is knocking. He is calling. He is waiting for you. He is the solution to your fears, anxieties, grief, and longings. You were created by Him and for Him.

He is coming soon.

Amen. So be it. Come, Lord Jesus.

Please don't forget your free gift (PDF):

*What in the World is Going On
(and What's Coming Next)?*

https://www.garyroe.com/what-in-the-world

RECEIVING JESUS AND HIS LIFE

*"Enter through the narrow gate. For wide is the gate
and broad is the road that leads to destruction, and
many enter through it. But small is the gate and
narrow the road that leads to life,
and only a few find it."*

- Jesus (Matthew 7:13-14)

You long to be loved.

You hunger for safety and significance.

You were designed for eternity.

You were made for a relationship with God.

Jesus came for you. He died on the cross for you. He conquered death for you.

He planned you. He created you. He knows who you truly are.

He has a plan for you. He wants to be with you. He wants you to be with Him forever.

He loves you.

He is with you right now.

He is waiting for you.

> *For all have sinned and fallen short of the glory of God.*
> *(Romans 3:23)*

All have sinned, including you. No one can earn their way to God. You cannot do anything to take away your own sin and save yourself.

> *For the wages of sin is death, but the free gift of*
> *God is eternal life in Jesus Christ our Lord.*
> *(Romans 6:23)*

We are all born physically alive but spiritually dead. We begin sinning early. We develop patterns of behavior to try and get our needs met apart from God.

You were born spiritually dead. Only God has eternal life. To be forgiven and have eternal life, you must let God save you. Neither forgiveness nor eternal life can be earned. Both are gifts. They can only be received.

> *But God demonstrates his own love for us in this:*
> *While we were still sinners, Christ died for us.*
> *(Romans 5:8)*

Jesus took all your sin and rebellion against God on Himself and died in your place. That's how much God loves you.

For it is by grace you have been saved, through
faith—and this is not from yourselves, it
is the gift of God— not by works,

so that no one can boast.

(Ephesians 2:8-9)

Jesus died for you and then conquered death. He is forgiveness and life. Receive Him. Trust Him, and Him alone, to save you.

Forgiveness and eternal life are both gifts. Jesus is the gift. He cannot be earned. He can only be received.

Please don't delay another moment. Trust Jesus now.

How do you do that?

You acknowledge that you're a sinner in need of forgiveness and salvation.

You acknowledge and believe that Jesus Christ came and died for you, in your place.

You acknowledge and believe that Jesus conquered death and rose from the dead.

You put your faith and trust in Christ and Christ alone to save you and bring you into a relationship with Himself.

"I tell you the truth; whoever hears my word and
believes Him who sent me has eternal life and will not
be condemned but has crossed over from death to life."

(John 5:24)

If you just trusted in Jesus and in Him alone for salvation, welcome to true life, real life, eternal life! You need to know that you are now and forever eternally secure.

You have heard Jesus' word. You believed in Him. You now <u>have</u> eternal life. You <u>have crossed over</u> from death to life.

> *We know that we are children of God, and that*
> *the whole world is under the control of the evil*
> *one. We know also that the Son of God has come*
> *and has given us understanding, so that we may*
> *know him who is true. And we are in him who*
> *is true by being in his Son Jesus Christ.*
>
> *He is the true God and eternal life.*
>
> *(1 John 5:19-20)*

Jesus Himself is life. He is eternal life. You now have <u>His life</u>. He now lives <u>in</u> you.

> *"My sheep listen to my voice; I know them, and they*
> *follow me. I give them eternal life, and they shall never*
> *perish; no one will snatch them out of my hand."*
>
> *(John 10:27-28)*

You are now forever His. You <u>have</u> eternal life. Nothing and no one can steal your salvation.

> *Therefore, there is now no condemnation*
> *for those who are in Christ Jesus...*
>
> *(Romans 8:1)*

Jesus took all your condemnation. He was condemned in your place. He died your death. You have now been given His eternal life. You are free.

> *Therefore, if anyone is in Christ, the new creation has come: The old has gone, the new is here! (2 Corinthians 5:17)*

You are now __in__ Christ. Christ is now __in__ you. You are a new creation. You have a new heart.

Christ is now your life. Daily life is now about being with Him, learning from Him, and following Him.

As soon as possible, please let someone else, another believer in Christ, know that you have trusted Christ. This will encourage you.

If you don't have a physical Bible, please get one. In the meantime, use an online Bible or Bible site. I would recommend reading the Gospel of John in the New Testament first.

If you're not already going to a good Bible-teaching, Jesus-focused church, begin searching for one.

Please feel free to reach out to me for input, help, and recommendations. You can contact me at **www.garyroe.com**.

I rejoice with you in your new life – in your new relationship with Jesus Christ! Welcome to His family!

Hear the voice of your Savior:

> *"I am the gate; whoever enters through me will be saved. They will come in and go out, and find pasture. The thief comes only to steal and kill and destroy;*

I have come that they may have life,
and have it to the full.

I am the good shepherd. The good shepherd
lays down his life for the sheep."

(John 10:9-11)

ADDITIONAL RESOURCES

Free on Gary's Website
Available at www.garyroe.com

GRIEF: 9 THINGS I WISH I HAD KNOWN

In this deeply personal and practical eBook, Gary shares nine key lessons from his own grief journeys. "This was so helpful! I saw myself on every page," said one reader. "I wish I had read this years ago," said another. Widely popular, this eBook has brought hope and comfort to thousands of grieving hearts.

THE GOOD GRIEF MINI-COURSE

Full of personal stories, inspirational content, and practical assignments, this 8-session email series is designed to help readers understand grief and deal with its roller-coaster emotions. Thousands have been through this course, which is now being used in support groups as well.

THE HOLE IN MY HEART:
TACKLING GRIEF'S TOUGH QUESTIONS

This eBook tackles some of grief's big questions: "How did this happen?" "Why?" "Am I crazy?" "Am I normal?" "Will this get any easier?" plus others. Written in the first person, it engages and comforts the heart.

I MISS YOU: A HOLIDAY SURVIVAL KIT

Thousands have downloaded this brief, easy-to-read, and very personal e-book. *I Miss You* provides some basic, simple tools on how to use holiday and special times to grieve well and love those around you.

Available at www.garyroe.com.

THE GOD AND GRIEF SERIES

GRIEF DEVOTIONALS

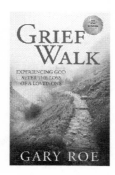

Grief Walk

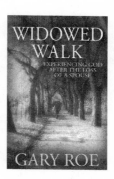

Widowed Walk

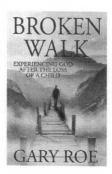

Broken Walk

ABOUT THE AUTHOR

Gary's story began with a childhood of mixed messages and sexual abuse. This was followed by other losses and numerous grief experiences.

Ultimately, a painful past led Gary into a life of helping wounded people heal and grow. A former college minister, missionary in Japan, entrepreneur in Hawaii, pastor, hospice chaplain, and grief counselor, he now serves as an author, speaker, Bible teacher, grief specialist, and grief coach.

In addition to *Soul Cry*, Gary is the author of more than 20 books, including the award-winning bestsellers *The Grief Guidebook, Shattered: Surviving the Loss of a Child, Comfort for the Grieving Spouse's Heart*, and *Aftermath: Picking Up the Pieces After a Suicide*. Gary's books have won four international book awards and have been named finalists seven times. He has been featured on Dr. Laura, Belief Net, the Christian Broadcasting Network, Wellness, Thrive Global, and other major media and has published well over 900 grief-related articles. Known for his engaging style and sense of humor, Gary is a Bible teacher and speaker at churches, conferences, and seminars.

Gary loves being a husband and father. He has seven adopted children. He enjoys hockey, corny jokes, good puns, and colorful Hawaiian shirts. Gary and his wife Jen and family live in Texas.

Visit Gary at **www.garyroe.com**.

AN URGENT PLEA

HELP OTHER WOUNDED, GRIEVING HEARTS

Dear Reader,

Others are hurting and grieving today. You can help.

How?

With a simple, heartfelt review.

Could you take a few moments and write a 1-3 sentence review of *Soul Cry* and leave it on the site you purchased the book from?

And if you want to help even more, you could leave the same review on the *Soul Cry* book page on Goodreads. com.

Your review counts and will help reach others who could benefit from this book.

Thanks for considering this. I read these reviews as well, and your comments and feedback assist me in producing more quality resources for grieving hearts.

Thank you!
Warmly,
Gary

Don't forget your free eBook (PDF):
What in the World is Going On
(And What's Coming Next)?
Download yours today:
https://www.garyroe.com/what-in-the-world